A Far Better Life

*Spiritual and Psychological Insights
from Jesus' Teaching*

JAMES G. FRIESEN

WIPF & STOCK · Eugene, Oregon

A FAR BETTER LIFE
Spiritual and Psychological Insights from Jesus' Teaching

Wipf & Stock
A Division of Wipf and Stock Publishers
199 W. 8th Ave., Suite 3
Eugene, OR 97401

www.wipfandstock.com

ISBN 13: 978-1-55635-912-5

Manufactured in the U.S.A.

If you seek the Lord your God, you will find him
if you look for him with all your heart and with all your soul.

taken from Deuteronomy 4:29, New International Version

Contents

Acknowledgments

THANKS TO DR. LEE Edward Travis, my advisor and mentor, for believing in me. His faith and vision are still alive in his students. Following his example, may we never cease to be amazed at what God has created.

Thanks to Dr. Dallas Willard, for his tireless dedication to God. After hearing an audio tape of a seminar that he presented, my spiritual life was not only renewed but gained direction. His hunger for truth is contagious.

And thanks to my former colleague, Dr. Jim Wilder. For twenty years I was privileged to learn from his observations every time we met. His life has shown a crystal clear desire to serve God, through critical thinking and compassion.

Part One

Learning

A Prelude

THE GIANT REDWOODS ARE found only in a few hidden groves, high on the western slopes of the Sierra Nevadas. My parents introduced me to those graceful giants, and I did the same for my children. I have re-visited them many times, and have noticed that first time viewers simply freeze in their tracks, stunned. They usually stand silently, catching their breath, and then snap a few photos which do not capture the stately trees' true magnificence. But later, back at home, they can hardly wait to tell their friends about what they have seen, and the words finally come pouring out.

"You've just got to see them for yourself! You cannot even *imagine* what it's like to walk among them. Those trees are staggeringly beautiful. They are these gorgeous, reddish-colored, velvet-like, humongous . . . . I really cannot tell you what it's like."

There is a copied picture that may give you a clue about how impossibly big they are in real life. In the book, *They Felled the Redwoods* (Hank Johnson, 1996), one of the pictures from early logging days shows the remaining stump of a felled tree. Fifty men are lined up to be photographed, all standing on top of the fallen giant's massive stump, and there is room for at least a hundred more. My written words are inadequate. You gotta' see it, and even then you may not believe it.

A tale is told in that book, on page 15, about how the redwoods were discovered. News came from Murphy's Camp, "a brawling, rip-roaring gold settlement . . . populated mainly by miners, gamblers, prostitutes and bandits." In 1852, Mr. Dowd, a hunter employed by some miners to furnish game, was tracking down a bear he had wounded, when he wandered into a giant redwood grove. "He found himself face to face with the largest trees that he had ever seen! He quite naturally lost all interest in the errant bear and rushed breathlessly back to camp, full of the news of his remarkable discovery. Unfortunately, no one at Murphy's would believe his tale;

many, in fact, thought he was drunk, and not a single person would go back with him to see the trees."

"Dowd was obviously a most resourceful individual. He bided his time for what seemed a reasonable period, then rushed into camp again and announced that he had just shot 'the largest grizzly bear that I ever saw in my life.' The bear, of course, was a fake. But the story was apparently more believable than the one about the trees had been, for this time Dowd was able to persuade a group of miners to accompany him into the woods. On the pretext of searching for the grizzly, he steered the party into the grove of giant trees. As the miners gaped in astonishment, Dowd yelled triumphantly, 'Now, boys, do you believe my story?'"

As is the case for first-timers in a redwood grove, Jesus' teaching will leave you amazed and silent. Expect to be surrounded by the extraordinary.

1

The Gathering

T HERE IS AN URGE within our souls to live a better life. Even at birth this desire is already our constant companion. It troubles our hearts and will not go away. Jesus' most comprehensive teaching, called *The Sermon on the Mount*, puts this problem on the table, and He presents His ideas in an easy-to-follow fashion. Jesus explains that the heart does not need to stay troubled. A far better life is reachable.

SETTING THE STAGE

If you are looking for an introduction to Jesus' teachings, this is where to find it. Here He explains how to live a life that is as good as it gets. The first step is establishing a spiritual foundation. The blueprint for that foundation is laid out in the sermon's introduction, called *The Beatitudes*. But before we unpack that teaching, let's set the stage.

Before Jesus began His ministry He went to the Jordan River to be baptized by John the Baptist, which showed the world that He was serious about following God. Unlike the other people being baptized that day, God singled out Jesus as He was emerging from the water, and the Spirit of God descended upon him like a dove. God's voice rang out, *"This is my beloved son, whom I love. I am very pleased with him."*

Can you imagine standing on the river's bank during that God-filled moment? I suppose that the people there were utterly caught by surprise. They certainly had to tell their friends what had happened, who immediately told their friends, and the story soon was passed from village to village.

"I saw the son of God today! And I heard God's voice at the river. And there was this dove—I've never seen anything like it."

"Perhaps you were mistaken. How can you be sure?"

"I wish I knew for certain. In a moment it was over."

"So tell me exactly what happened."

No doubt, quiet little debates soon sprang up. Put yourself there. Who would believe that God's voice would come out of nowhere and say that this is His son? But there were many witnesses. The story definitely commanded people's attention.

Everyone in the whole region soon had heard something about it, and people were at the very least, curious, even if they remained somewhat skeptical. They wanted to know more, so they tried to find Him. But following the baptism, the Holy Spirit had immediately led Jesus away to the desert for 40 days of prayer and fasting. By the time He returned, everyone was wondering just where He had gone. Those who had heard God's voice at His baptism could not stop thinking about the whole spectacle.

Jesus came back from the desert ready to begin his work. He visited the local synagogues and delivered this challenging message everywhere He went:

> You can turn your life around because God is right there by your side, available to help you with any problem that comes up. (Matt. 4:17)[1]

He soon took up residence in Capernaum, a small town on the shore of Lake Galilee, a mere stone's throw away from where the Jordan River enters into that large, serene body of water. Just behind the scattered remains of that town today, you can see the broad, gradually sloping hillside effortlessly making its way up to the skyline, a few miles away. A short walk up the side of that hill brings you to a spacious, inspiring lookout point—a perfect setting for the most compelling sermon ever.

As Jesus was delivering His message in the local synagogues, He healed sicknesses of every sort wherever he went. As you might imagine, folks could not help but talk about these miracles. The lives of people they all knew, neighbors who had been hobbled by chronic conditions for years, were being transformed.

---

1. Translation notes: The word used here, often translated as, "repent" means "to turn around and go in the opposite direction." The phrase used here by Jesus, "the kingdom of the heavens," refers to the Father's availability. He is "in the heavens, the air around you." See *The Divine Conspiracy*, chapter 4, by Dallas Willard, for a fuller explanation. This is how some translations record this teaching: "Repent, for the kingdom of heaven is at hand." That is a direct translation, and does not convey the idea that Jesus was describing, nor why this simple message is so compelling. We will examine this teaching further in the next section.

Word of these miracles began to spread. "The Son of God would do that, don't you think? I believe it *was* the voice of God that we heard when He was baptized."

The public's interest soared because people's lives were being dramatically changed. It helps to keep in mind that in those days, *person to person* was the only way that stories could spread. The word "news" was not yet invented. Newspapers and the mass media were centuries away. People had to rely on each other to stay up-to-date. If a miracle took place it would be the big story at the local synagogue, and it would be the number one topic in every discussion. After all, why would people want to talk about what happened down at the lake when there were miracles to talk about? People took great care back then to repeat important stories accurately. They listened intently and precisely relayed every little detail to family and friends. Everyone was a news gatherer and a news reporter. You can be certain that everyone carefully went over the stories about Jesus, and passed them on.

Before long His little town was swarming with the oddest collection of diseased folks, epileptics and demon-possessed people ever. They descended on His community from quite a distance. More and more people kept showing up, and all of their illnesses were healed by the man whom God had called His son at the Jordan River. Folks began to wonder out loud whether this might *truly* be God's son. The scene around Jesus soon went from a bunch of ill, grumpy people to those who were no longer ill, and certainly no longer grumpy. They were clamoring with life, exuberant about what Jesus had done for them.

"I was sure I was dying, but I met Him and now I feel like a new person. I cannot thank Him enough!"

You may know some people who were dramatically changed by God. Did they stay quiet? Of course not. Once people have had a taste of God's goodness, they start to overflow and must talk about it. What Jesus had created was a whole town full of transformed people in that condition. Radiant and laughing, the joy was not containable.

Jesus' reputation was spreading by now like a Southern California wildfire. The "swarms" of seekers soon became "crowds." People were coming together from quite a distance, hoping to see Him or meet Him or at least, hear His teaching for themselves.

Those already healed were being joined by their friends, who were, very likely, hoping that He could also help them with their problems, big and small. They were certain that this was a "once in a lifetime" opportunity. *The Gospel of Luke*, chapter 6, describes the scene, just as the people were starting to gather around Him: "All the crowd was seeking to touch Him, because power went forth from Him and cured them all."

That sentence really leaps out at me. The healing arts were not very advanced in those days, and perhaps half of the people who approached Him were feeling ill. Even if only 10% of them were not feeling well, when "power went forth from Him and cured them all," you had better believe that those who were feeling better began to talk about it.

"My pain vanished!"

"Same here!"

Some were giggling and smiling, and some could only stand in a moment of quiet disbelief. After they were all cured, you can bet that they were ready to listen to the man with the healing power. He had earned the right to be heard.

When Jesus saw so many people gathering, He took a little walk up the hillside to find a place where there was more room. While He was getting started, more and more folks were huddling around, scooting in as close as they could. Everyone became still, as though their very lives depended on hearing His every word. No event in history could compare with that scene on the hillside.

Jesus began to talk with them, looking out over the expansive lake. It was a bit like an amphitheatre setting. While He was speaking, people could glance up and see across the huge lake, where the distant mountain range stretched out beyond the horizon, as His timeless truths came to them. Eternity was meeting infinity. Hearts were ready to be transformed. It was a moment like no other. Jesus spoke to them from His heart to theirs.

The great gathering was treated to a profound, yet simple teaching. None of them had brought along their notepads and pencils, and nobody had a tape recorder so that His words could be transcribed later. As He began to talk to them, Jesus started with the basics and built His ideas progressively, so that they all could easily understand. He kept His train of thought very simple, and included a few examples that explained how their lives could be completely changed by opening up to the Kingdom of the Heavens. His listeners were transfixed.[2]

---

2. You will find this sermon in *The Gospel According to Matthew*, chapters 5 through 7. Dr. Dallas Willard's brilliant chapter about *The Sermon on the Mount* in his book, *The Divine Conspiracy*, has been a rich resource in shaping my thinking about this sermon.

As we take a look at what Jesus taught that day, please go over the ideas more than once, discuss them in groups, think about them on your own, pray about them and let them grow on you. Go back and review them regularly. But don't ignore them. You do so at your peril. You will discover that this teaching addresses many of life's major sticking points, including hopelessness, contempt, lust, forgiveness and worry. Jesus talks about these and other heart battles that prevent people from living a far better life.

THE KINGDOM OF THE HEAVENS

One study guideline that I learned in seminary has helped me with this sermon: "Take a look at the original text." *The New Testament* is taken from ancient Greek manuscripts. Translators try to match the words from those early texts with English words, and capture the intent of the original ideas. Bible translators are always asking themselves, "What did this group of words *mean* back then? What *ideas* do these words convey?"

I have learned enough about the Greek language to read the Greek words in those manuscripts. That is not enough. I need help figuring out the original meaning from people who have delved, more deeply than I, into the language and culture. Dr. Willard and Dr. Bruce[3] have done just that, and have gotten me closer to what some of the sermon's key words and phrases meant in that time and place.

When we try to grasp what Jesus was teaching about "the kingdom of the heavens," we cannot afford to miss what that particular phrase meant. It is a key that unlocks this sermon. I cannot stress too strongly how important it is to understand what this phrase meant in that language and culture.

Jesus had already been preaching a simple message in synagogues throughout the area, and it was about the Kingdom of the Heavens: *"You can turn your lives around because the Kingdom of the Heavens is at hand. God is right there by your side, available to help you with any problem that comes up."*

Jesus did *not* use the term, "the Kingdom of Heaven," which is what Bible translators often conclude that Jesus must have meant, even though the Greek manuscripts clearly use the term, "the Kingdom of the Heavens." It is most unfortunate that only those people who have the Greek text are able to see that the word used in this teaching is really "heavens." The

You may want to read Dr. Willard's book in order to get better acquainted with his ideas.

3. Dallas Willard, *The Divine Conspiracy* and F. F. Bruce, *The Hard Sayings of Jesus.*

Greek manuscript says "heavens," *plural*. That means something entirely different from "heaven," *singular*.

Dr. Willard explains the difference. When people referred to "the heavens" in Jesus' culture, it meant "the air around you; your living space." Keeping that in mind, Jesus' message is best translated like this: "God is with you. His kingdom includes your living space. He can help you with anything, any time." That simple message is the meat and potatoes of a spiritual life—where the rubber meets the road. You don't have to climb every mountain or reach for the sky or follow every rainbow—God is with you all of the time, right there in your living space. People could not ignore His message then, and that is still the case today. It is where Christian experience begins—God is with us.

Before you prematurely dismiss this interpretation about the Kingdom of the Heavens, please take a look at the way Jesus used the words "heaven" and "heavens" a little later in the same sermon, when He was teaching about prayer—*The Lord's Prayer*. It begins by using the *plural form of the word*: "Our Father in the *heavens* . . . ."

In my growing up years I pictured a stately God who is somewhere far away, up there in heaven, sitting quietly on His throne whenever I prayed, "Our Father, who art in heaven." Prayers of that sort take on the quality of a long distance telephone call. "Please hear me from down here on earth, Father, and take a few minutes off from whatever is going on up there in heaven to answer my prayer."

However, that is really different from what Jesus was telling the hillside gathering about talking things over with the Father. Jesus was giving them good news. "God is with you! He is in your living space. He is not somewhere far, far away. God is available right where you are, so when you pray, talk to the Father who is presently with you."

When Jesus was teaching about "our Father in the heavens" He was describing someone who is right beside us. Tears filled my eyes when I first corrected my false notion that God is far away, up there somewhere in heaven, and I truly welcomed Him into my living space. What a *spiritual* breakthrough that was for me. "God is with me" *is* the good news. *It is the spiritual foundation for a better life.*

A few lines later in *The Lord's Prayer* we find Jesus teaching us to ask God to let His will be done in our lives, just as His will is done in heaven. Strikingly, Jesus uses the *singular form of the word* at this point—"heaven."

That is a place where God's will is carried out all of the time. Do you see how this is different from "heavens," which is the plural form of the word?

Jesus used the plural form ("our Father in the heavens") when He spoke about God's presence, and then in the same prayer He used the singular form ("may your will be done in heaven") when He spoke about letting the Father carry out His will in our lives, just as His will is carried out in heaven.

That pretty well clinches the point. Everything that He taught that day can be put into practice because God's presence can help you make it happen. You cannot create a far better life alone, but it can happen if you welcome the Father into your living space.

You will need His hands-on guidance in order to put this sermon into practice. When, for example, Jesus taught a little later that we are not to worry at all about our lives (Matt. 6:25), we will find that does not work unless He is available to help. It is precisely "living in the Kingdom of the Heavens" that gives us the confidence that God will take care of us, so that we do not have to "worry about our lives." If you are supposed to stop worrying on your own it would be like trying to lift yourself up by your shoestrings. The good news is that God is with you, so you really do not have to be concerned at all about your life. He's got you covered. You're good to go. No worries.

The Sermon on the Mount is about living differently. Your life will completely turn around if this message changes your heart and directs your actions. As Jesus' teaching took shape on the hillside that day, the gathering began to see that He was telling them *how to change everything.* The Father's guidance is available, and He will be with you in the middle of your day, during your most difficult problems. Whether it is overcoming hopelessness, contempt, lust, dishonesty or worry, Jesus was speaking to people who heard Him say, "By living in the Kingdom of the Heavens you will be able to make this happen."

The Father will help you in every personal encounter and in every task that you face. He will give you the wisdom to act according to His wishes. You can take each step, surrounded by the Father's presence. He will give you guidance. Your life will be far better because of his consistent availability. Jesus' teaching brings the Father from *out there* to *right here.* We are not left to face life's decisions alone, because He is *at hand* all of the time. And what happens when God is *at hand*? People can open up about their troubled hearts, and let the Kingdom of the Heavens satisfy their souls.

2

The Sermon on the Mount: A Reader-Friendly Version

Here is the message that Jesus had been preaching wherever He went. It was a simple, compelling message, almost too good to be true.[1]

You can turn your life around because God is right there by your side, available to help you with any problem that comes up

(Matthew 4:17).[2]

THE BEATITUDES—THE FIRST STEP

We read Jesus' opening words of this sermon in *Matthew*, chapter 5.

> 3 *God blesses those who are spiritually broken. He is lovingly available, moment by moment, as each problem comes up, to help them establish a new spiritual life.*
>
> 4 *God blesses those who are overcome with sadness. His immediate comfort is always available.*
>
> 5 *God blesses those who hang in there when they are treated unfairly. He will help them win in the end.*

---

1. This chapter contains the author's paraphrase of the sermon, based on the Greek text. Jesus' words, which are italicized, work together in ideas and in groups of ideas that build as the sermon develops. The author's non-italicized comments are included, which makes this different than reading "translated words." This sermon contains a wealthy stream of ideas, and that makes a direct translation very limited. It may help the reader to think of the italicized words as a paraphrase, and the rest as a commentary that links the sermon's ideas together. Chapter 3 is called "Approaching *The Sermon on the Mount.*" It explains in more detail how these ideas came together in their present form.

2. See footnote 1, page 3.

6 God blesses those who try very hard to live correctly.[3] His guidance will bring them peace as they make daily decisions.

7 God blesses those who are seriously drained from being merciful. His loving presence will keep them filled up.

8 God blesses those who deeply long to stay pure. As they keep their eyes on Him, He will guide them.

9 God blesses those who are devoted to making peace. His children are peacemakers, and He will join them in their efforts.

10 God blesses those who are persecuted because they follow Him. He is available to give them direction, moment by moment, as each problem comes up. His availability is the cornerstone of their spiritual foundation.

Jesus immediately begins to build on the closing *Beatitude*, introducing the idea that there is something about God's closeness that is a great help during persecution.

11–12 God will bless you while you are being insulted, persecuted and slandered because you follow me. Get ready for a big surprise. Great joy will come to you while you are being persecuted, because of His presence (in the "heavens"). God has always been close to people, like the prophets, who follow Him despite opposition. His presence will give you great joy.

Here is the core idea that Jesus was sharing when He delivered *The Beatitudes*.

I can tell how hard life is for you. You may believe that God will never pour out His goodness onto you in any meaningful way. Trust me. You can live a far better life if you open up to His presence. He is always available to help you, especially during hard times. When you are spiritually broken, overcome with sadness, treated unfairly, trying to live a better life, seriously drained, deeply longing, overwhelmed and persecuted, be encouraged—God is at work all around you. Your heart does not need to stay troubled. Let yourself enjoy His presence. It is wonderful to be with the Father. By welcoming Him into your living space, you will enter into the Kingdom of the Heavens.

---

3. A translation note: "Righteous" means "living correctly."

PREPARING YOUR HEART

The Beatitudes challenge people to welcome the Father into their daily lives, and thereby enter into the Kingdom of the Heavens. That is the first step. Preparing your heart to receive His guidance is second, so we next find Jesus talking about that.

Here is an overview of the sermon that shows how the "Preparing Your Heart" section fits in. Immediately following *The Beatitudes*, Jesus covers six problem areas that can defeat your heart. This section builds up to the sermon's climax—*The Lords Prayer*. After that, the remainder of the sermon applies each of the "Preparing Your Heart" lessons to daily living, in a section that can be called, "Living from a Transformed Heart." Not only does that section shed light on living, it uses each of the six heart-preparation areas as building blocks, applying them to the areas covered in the second half of the sermon. Jesus prepared people for the sermon's end from the beginning: He covered six areas of heart preparation in the first half of the sermon, and each area needs to be worked on in order to be ready to obey Jesus' teaching in the second half. The ideas are nicely interwoven and fit together without any loose ends.

As we begin this section, please keep the sermon flow in mind. Pay close attention to the Preparing Your Heart section, because without that you will not be ready to receive His guidance in daily living. A wounded heart can create too much static to hear God clearly. Jesus takes up hopelessness as His first heart-related target, because the hopelessness wound is a heart killer. His approach is remarkably encouraging.

Hopelessness

13 You may feel like salt on the ground. Salt is only valuable if it stays salty, but if it loses its saltiness, how can it be made salty again? It is no longer good for anything, except to be discarded and trampled by men. I really do understand that you sometimes feel like an old pile of discarded, trampled salt. If you lose life's richness, you may believe that you will never get it back.[4]

---

4. Some teachers believe that Jesus is telling his listeners here that it is wonderful to be "the salt of the earth." That is not what the text is saying. Much of their salt came from the Dead Sea, and scraping it from the ground's surface could make the salt completely worthless. Discarded salt is what Jesus is speaking of here, and it is not a good thing to be "discarded salt on the ground." Further discussion is found in chapter 3, "Approaching *The Sermon on the Mount*," notation 7.

14 But here is something encouraging to keep in mind. You are the light that shines throughout the world, and you will make a difference everywhere you go. You will carry God with you. Like a city on a hill, you will not be hidden. 15 People do not light a lamp and put it under a bowl. Instead they put it on a stand so that it will give light to everyone in the house. 16 In the same way let your light shine before men so that they may see your good deeds and glorify the Father who helps you with everything. Don't give up. You will make a difference, and God will receive all of the credit.

The Father's Guidance vs. Rules

There was a tradition that Jesus needed to speak about with the hillside gathering before He covered the next four heart preparation topics. "Teachers" were telling them that they need rules, in addition to what was revealed in "the law and the prophets." God's everlasting law, revealed in the Old Testament, goes hand-in-hand with His approach. Jesus exposed, in this teaching, the self-defeating nature of the many, many man-made rules. He made this introductory point in order to speak authoritatively about the four heart preparation areas that follow. He needed to free people's hearts from "the rules approach." Rules do not tell you how to live. A healthy heart, attuned to God, will direct your actions from the inside out. That is His approach, and it is consistent with God's revealed law.

17 Do not think that I have come to abolish the law or the prophets. I have not come to abolish them, but to fulfill them. 18 I tell you the truth, until "heaven" and earth disappear, not the smallest part of the law will by any means disappear. Follow the laws. 19 Anyone who breaks the least of these commandments and teaches others to do the same will be called the least in the Kingdom of the "Heavens." God will not guide you to break His commandments. 20 But keep this in mind. Extra rules are the problem. Unless you live even more correctly than the teachers and the Pharisees, who have completely devoted their lives to following extra rules that are not directly in the law and the prophets, you will not be able to enter the Kingdom of the "Heavens." Some of their rules make no sense, and can take your life in the wrong direction.

"Entering the Kingdom of the Heavens" is opening up every area of your life and counting on Him for guidance in every one of those areas. In the Kingdom of the Heavens the Father is right there, and His guidance is better than any list of rules. He will not lead you to break God's commandments, but He will help you to see when the extra rules, provided and strictly followed by rule-makers, are wrong.

Rather than seeking lists of rules, seek the Father who wants to meet you in your heart. He sees your heart and that helps Him know how you are doing, what you need and how He should guide you. The ongoing problem with your heart is that it frequently gets clogged up with the aftereffects of wounds. Healing is a must.

A wounded heart blocks God from giving you guidance. It propels you into self-directed deeds because you are on your own, cut off from His guidance. In that position, you may not be able to see whether a particular rule is right. In order for His guidance to work, do not rely on rules but rely on a heart that is prepared to hear from God. You will need His guidance to keep your heart from being directed by wounds like contempt, lust, dishonesty, retaliation and false righteousness. The list could have included other issues, no doubt, but Jesus explains how these can sneak into your life and clog up your heart.

Contempt

21 As you know, it was said long ago, "Do not murder," and "Whoever murders will not escape judgment." 22 But I tell you that anyone who is angry with his brother will not escape judgment, anyone who speaks contemptuously to his brother should be censured by the elders, and anyone who calls his brother crazy—disowning him—will face hell fire. If anger is the problem you dare not ignore it. It leads to contempt, which can escalate, causing long-lasting family scars. Murder is certainly not where problems start. That is a "rules approach." You need to deal with anger before it begins to direct your heart. That is my approach.

23 Catch contempt problems early. If you are offering a gift to God at the altar and remember that you are having a problem with a brother, 24 leave your gift there, work things out with your brother and then offer your gift to God. Eliminating contempt in its early stages, especially in family relationships, is more important than following religious rules.

25 Here is one more area where contempt can creep into your life— legal matters. Settle things quickly with your adversary so that you are not taken before a judge, who could put you into prison. Contempt can lead to awful outcomes in court. 26 There is nothing

worth going to court about if it will jeopardize relationships. Avoid legal fights because they foster long-lasting contempt, and can seriously clog up your heart.

Lust

27 It was also said long ago that you should not commit adultery. That is another "rules approach." Adultery is not where problems begin. 28 Here is my approach. Anyone who looks lustfully at a woman has already committed adultery in his heart. 29 It is better to gouge your eye out than to let lust lead you to hell. 30 It is better to cut your right hand off than to let lust lead you to hell. Lust can definitely get you into serious trouble. Do whatever it takes to deal with lust, because it can destroy your heart.

31 It was also said long ago that it is allowed to dismiss your wife if you give her a proper divorce certificate. That rule does not deal with the underlying problem—lust. 32 I say that, apart from adultery, you should not simply dismiss your wife, just because you can do so according to your rules. That will certainly lead to lust-related problems for everyone involved. Search your heart before you so easily choose divorce. The Father's guidance is essential.

Dishonesty

33 It was also said long ago that you should not break an oath that you make to the Lord. We all know that there is a list of rules about how to convince people that you are really telling the truth by stating your oath in just the right way. That is a bunch of foolishness. 34-35 You should not have to make oaths of any sort. You do not have to swear by "heaven" or by the earth or by Jerusalem or by anything else in the list of rules about making oaths. 36 You will not seem any more believable just because you follow rules. 37 Here is my approach. You need to be transparently honest. That is all you need to concern yourself with. Integrity comes from the heart, and people will know whether you are telling the truth. If you even exaggerate, that is from the evil one. You will not convince people by exaggeration. Your heart will tell the world, through your actions, whether you are being honest.

Retaliation

38 It was also said that under certain conditions retaliation is allowed. That "rules approach" is wrong. Here is my approach. 39-42 I say that you should not fight back against an evil person. If an evil person strikes you a second time, steals from you a second time, repeatedly pressures you for money or causes you unnecessary physical hardship, do not retaliate. By holding your retaliation in check, an evil person's violence will expose his evil intent for all to see, and you will be totally exonerated. Your steadfast heart will win in the long run, as was mentioned in the third "Beatitude." More importantly, you will promote peace, and the Father will help you with that, as was mentioned in the seventh "Beatitude."⁵ Those "Beatitudes" will help you to keep your heart free from retaliation, as you seek the Father's guidance.

43 It was also said, "You should love your neighbor and hate your enemy." 33 If you follow that rule, everyone loses. Here is my approach. I say to love your enemies and pray for those who persecute you, 45 because that shows you are sons of the Father—you are following His guidance (in the "heavens").⁶ If you want to show yourselves to be sons of the Father, remember this in all of your relationships: God is "perfect" when it comes to being generous to everyone.⁷ He pours out plenty of sun and nourishing rain on those who love him and those who don't. 46 If you reserve special favors for those who give you special favors, you are no better than tax collectors, who gouge people's income as a way of life! 47 If you are only nice to your family, you are no better than heathens who do not know God at all.

48 Be equally generous to friends and foes alike, just as the Father is generous to everyone all of the time. That shows you are following the Father's guidance (in the "heavens"). You will not be able to fool anyone about what is in your heart, whether it is retaliation or generosity. That will tell people whether you are a son of the evil one or of the Father in the heavens.

---

5. Here you can see how Jesus' earlier comments are being built upon as the sermon develops. When He teaches about forgiveness, just after The Lord's Prayer, we will find Him again building upon what He has said here.

6. Remember, "in the heavens" means that he is with you, so when your generosity reflects his character, that shows he is with you, leading you to be generous.

7. This idea comes from *The Hard Sayings of Jesus*, by F. F. Bruce, page 74. You will find a fuller discussion in chapter 3, "Approaching *The Sermon on the Mount*," notation 4.

False Righteousness

> *6:1 Be very careful not to pretend to be a good person, hoping to draw attention to yourself through religious acts that appear "righteous." You will not fool the Father. He sees your heart, and your empty religious acts will not please Him at all. You will not receive what you expect from Him. You will lose everything.*
>
> *2 First of all, when you give to the needy do not announce your generosity with trumpets, acting as though you are in a theater production.*[8] *Your only glory will come from those who pat you on the back for a good performance. 3 Your Father who sees in secret will reward you if you keep quiet about your generous gifts to the poor. 4 In the end, if your heart is right when it comes to generosity, you will find favor with God.*
>
> *5 Another example where false righteousness can mislead you is in your prayer life. You will not gain God's favor with theater-like productions about praying, whether in church or out in public. Your only reward will be what you receive because you performed well. 6 Instead, avoid showing off when you pray. It is best to be completely alone. The Father who sees you in secret will repay you for your heart's prayers—those that are directed to Him, without seeking anyone's approval. If your heart is really seeking God you will not be seeking people's attention through acts of false righteousness.*

The wealth of knowledge about the heart that Jesus shares here is truly vast. His words open a door to see the heart at the deepest level ever revealed. The heart is where people meet God. Jesus makes it very clear that the heart is a battleground, and your identity will go to the victor. If you lose a battle to hopelessness, contempt, lust, dishonesty, retaliation or false righteousness, you will be acting like somebody who does not even know the Father. His guidance would not lead you to act like that. Whenever you lose control and are blocked from receiving His guidance, that is how you can tell that you are in the middle of a heart battle.

Let us take a look at an example which Jesus used in the "Contempt" section, where He highlighted a particular heart battle. If you completely lose it with your brother, call him names and viciously tell him you hope you never see him again, that fit of nastiness will change you at your core. You will not feel like the same person afterwards. Unresolved contempt

---

8. A translation note: The word that is often translated as "a hypocrite" can also mean "an actor."

toward him will seethe from everything you say, and you could very well turn into a totally nasty person. You could become like someone who does not even know God. When you lose heart battles like this, not only do you forget who you are, but things may escalate and you may eventually lose control of your whole life. Jesus spoke about heart battles in urgent terms. People absolutely need the Father's help, or the battles will surely be lost.

It is becoming more obvious, as Jesus continues, that preparing a heart can be a long-term project. There is often a lot of healing and transformation ahead, and that can take quite a while. Winning each battle is crucial, but winning the war for your heart may find you fighting many battles, which will require devotion and unwavering commitment.

Jesus is asking his listeners, "Who are you really? Are you going to let hopelessness, contempt, lust, dishonesty, retaliation and false righteousness tell you who you are? If so, that is living from your hurt. You know that you've got problems in at least some of those areas. Are you tired of losing heart battles? You need to start talking things over with the Father. He will be your constant companion as you learn to live from a transformed heart."

TALKING THINGS OVER WITH THE FATHER

As is the case for many Middle Eastern teachings, the main point for this sermon comes in the middle, which is different from our culture, where it is most often found at the end.[9] Jesus is truly hitting His stride right here, and is making a kind of summary statement in *The Lord's Prayer*. He lets the gathering know exactly how they are to carry on conversations with the Father who is always with them.

The Lord's Prayer mentions, or at least alludes to, some of the topics that Jesus has already spoken about: God is with you right where you are; honor is to go to God, not us; He is to guide everything in your life; and He can help you with false righteousness, lust and dishonesty. Jesus also includes some issues soon to appear in the sermon, including forgiveness, peacefulness and developing loving relationships. These are all identified as areas that you should be talking over with the Father on a regular basis. That is the essential ingredient to make it all work. You will either talk about these areas with the Father as they come up in your daily life, or you will fail to put Jesus' teaching into practice. Your heart will need some

---

9. See *Poet and Peasant*, by Kenneth Ewing Bailey.

gentle assistance in the transformation process, and you will find that His companionship is essential.

> *7 When you pray do not act like those who do not know about the Father's guidance. They do not pray about the right issues. They believe that if they pray long enough, they will eventually get through to God. 8 You do not have to pray like that, because your Father knows what you need before you ask. You can get to the right issues with Him. 9 Pray like this when you talk things over with your Father.*
>
> *"Our Father who is right here beside me (in the "heavens"), let Your name receive honor, not mine. 10 Please take control in every area of my life and guide me here on earth, just as You are in control of everything in "heaven." 11 Please help me not to worry about my daily bread. 12 Forgive me for my offenses in the same way that I forgive the offenses of others. 13 Lead me away from lust, and deliver me from being dishonest, like the evil one."*

So far this sermon has covered the availability of the Father and how your heart needs to be prepared, so that you will be able to receive His guidance when you are in the middle of heart battles. Six kinds of heart wounds have been covered, and each of them can stand in the way of living a better life, so they will need the Father's personal attention. There have also been a few reminders that the Father's presence is amazing and wonderful, and we have just heard Jesus describe how important it is to talk everything over with the Father, who is a constant companion. Jesus now turns His attention from overcoming heart wounds to living a better life, precisely because those wounds no longer stand in the way. During the remainder of the sermon He presents daily living problems that require a transformed heart and some "here and now" guidance from the Father. That is what it takes to "put His teaching into practice." Jesus brings up forgiveness as the first problem area.

LIVING FROM A TRANSFORMED HEART

Forgiveness and Your Heart

> *14 If you forgive others when they sin against you, your Father who is right by your side (in the "heavens") will forgive you.[10] 15 If you do not forgive the offenses of others, He will not forgive your offenses.*

---

10. Jesus provided heart preparation for this teaching, earlier in the sermon, in the "Retaliation" teaching, in chapter 5:38–48.

He knows whether you have a forgiving heart, and cannot guide you
if your heart is tainted with unforgiveness.

Forgiveness does not start with "how to forgive." It starts with overcoming spiritual brokenness, which takes us back to the first *Beatitude*. After we have welcomed the Father to help us with our spiritual brokenness—identifying where we need to be forgiven—He will show up and be ready to help us with forgiving others.

Here is one major sticking point in helping people to think correctly about forgiveness. When someone has wrongly inflicted pain it will interfere with the wounded person's life until the wound has been healed. That unhealed wound can cause a heart to remain unsettled, due to pain and the resulting thoughts of retaliation. Heart healing must take place, or the festering wound that urges retaliation can block forgiveness. In such a case, the person can falsely believe that because the pain is still there, forgiveness has not yet been reached. It *is* reached when a person refuses to retaliate, even if the pain remains.

Here is a second sticking point. Much of the time people do not have a definition for forgiveness, and that creates a lot of confusion. Here is the best definition I have heard: "Forgiveness is not a feeling. It is the decision to not retaliate." With this definition in mind, you can see the progression that Jesus is outlining. People can start by inviting the Father to help them with their spiritual brokenness, and then with His guidance they can seek healing for the wounds that urge retaliation. That clears the way to receive the Father's guidance in relationships, which go better without the urge to retaliate.

As you can see, the hillside gathering was not ready to hear about forgiveness before they had learned these two earlier lessons: The Father is available, and you need to know how to talk things over with the Father in order to win heart battles. It is not coincidental that the forgiveness section of this sermon follows those lessons. Living with the Father guiding your heart leads to success with forgiveness. If you are stuck in retaliation mode, that probably means you are living from your hurt. In that case, your heart will need some healing before the Father can guide.

Genuineness and Your Heart

16 Do not make a big theatrical production about how much you suffer when you fast, or the audience's approval will be your only reward.[11] Drawing attention to yourself is foolish, and trying to look good never works. 17-18 Do not fast in order to look religious. When you fast be as cheerful as possible, so that no one will know when you are fasting. The Father who sees everything will reward you. He knows what is in your heart. You do not have to impress Him by acting religious.

19 You have a lot of heart work ahead if you are devoted to collecting treasures here on earth. Those treasures will eventually be destroyed by moths or rust, or they may be stolen by thieves. They will soon be worthless, and nobody will be impressed. 20 You should be devoted to collecting treasures in "heaven." Seek whatever has eternal value. 21 You will not be able to hide what is in your heart. People will be able to see what you really collect—external treasures or eternal treasures.

22 You also have a lot of heart work ahead if you are not genuine about your devotion to God, in every area of your life. 23 Your outlook always needs to be attuned to whatever has eternal value. How great is the darkness that comes when your outlook is tainted with evil.

24 In a nutshell, this is what you need to know about genuineness and your heart: Nobody can serve two masters. You will not fool people with appearances, whether you try to act religious or attain great wealth. Your heart will declare who you are. Be genuine. If you are devoted to appearances, do not think for a moment that your heart is okay. You cannot serve the master of appearances and the master who sees your heart. It does not work to live your life in the light only part of the time.

Peacefulness and Your Heart

Jesus next turns to worry, which He had briefly mentioned in His teaching about prayer.[12] Here Jesus builds on an idea richly developed in *The Beatitudes*, namely, that the Father is ready to help, so we should learn to

---

11. Jesus provided heart preparation for this teaching, earlier in the sermon, in the "Dishonesty" teaching, in chapter 5:33–37.

12. Jesus provided heart preparation for this teaching, earlier in this sermon, in the "Hopelessness" teaching, in chapter 5:13–16.

count on Him all of the time. Overcoming hopelessness is also essential in order to deal with worry.

> 25 *Worry will not lead you to anything that has eternal value. To worry about your life—what you eat and what you wear—will get you nowhere. Your life is more important than externals, like food and clothes, for example.*

> 26 *Do not worry about your life. Look at the birds of the air ("heaven"). They get along just fine relying on God's care. They do not spend their lives storing up food, trying to prepare for an uncertain future, yet the Father takes care of them. Can you not see that the Father who is at your side (in the "heavens") places a much higher value on you than on birds? You need to count on Him. He will provide for you.*

> 27 *Do not worry about how you look. Can any of you grow a single inch taller by worrying? 28 Or take this as another example. What good can come from worrying about wearing the right clothes? They are external. The lilies of the field illustrate God's care. 29 Solomon himself was not that well dressed! 30 If God provides those lilies as a beautiful covering for the grasses of the field, which are here today and gone tomorrow, can you not trust that He will provide a suitable covering for you? Your faith must be really small if you cannot believe that He will provide for you.*

> 31 *Do not worry about food and clothing. 32 People who do not know about the Father's guidance (in the "heavens") seek after those things, but He is right beside you and knows just what you need. 33 Seek to be constantly in His presence. He will help you make good decisions each day.*

> 34 *It all comes down to believing that the Father will take care of you. Do not worry at all about tomorrow, even though you could find enough evil to worry about in every "tomorrow" if you tried. Drop your worries. You can count on Him to take care of you.*

Loving Relationships and Your Heart

Jesus' ideas continue to build.[13] What He has said about forgiveness, genuineness and worry are added to in this "Loving Relationships" section. These teachings all help with the daily life problems that complicate relationships.

---

13. Jesus provided heart preparation for this teaching, earlier in the sermon, in the "Contempt" and "Lust" teachings, found in chapter 5:21–32.

The Sermon on the Mount: *A Reader-Friendly Version*

7:1-2 When you judge others as being inferior, you are the inferior one. It is better to honestly work on your own spiritual brokenness, so that you will bring humility into relationships. Judging people pushes them away.

3 You must look at your own faults, not others.' When you are critical of the sawdust speck in your brother's eye, you may as well have a whole wooden beam in your own eye! 4-5 How ridiculous it is to try to help your brother with a speck in his eye while a beam is in yours! Take charge of your own life, not others.' Keep your heart healthy and you will be able to relate better.

6 Be careful not to push religion on people. In all of your relationships preserve what is holy, but do not fight with people about who is right. As the last "Beatitude" put it, you may very well be persecuted. Things could get out of hand. It could become as dangerous as trying to retrieve a holy book from a pack of vicious dogs or retrieving precious pearls from a herd of swine. You could be seriously persecuted—torn to pieces. Try not to be too confrontational about my teaching.

7-8 Instead, let your relationships be built on genuine qualities. You will find fulfillment in relationships that are based on a deep interest in each other. Be up front and clear, and ask people for what you need. That is a trustworthy approach. And seek to cooperate with them. That is also good. And knock on their door—take initiative and make things happen. These are trustworthy principles that will help you build loving relationships.

9-11 Do not try to manipulate or fool people. Seek the Father's help to stay honest in your relationships. Follow His example. He is not like a father who would fool his son. Like when a boy asks for bread, a father could put a smooth, round stone on his plate, trying to fool him a little, and tell him it is a roll. Or when a boy asks for a fish to eat, he could try to fool him by giving him a snake. What kind of a father would mislead his son like that? Even the worst parents know how to give good gifts to their children. The Father who is always by your side (in the "heavens") will surely not fool you if you request anything of Him. You can rely on Him to provide answers for tough relationship questions.

12 It is crucial to treat people in a way that does not make them feel inferior, yet recognizes that if you confront them, things could get out of hand. Understanding people correctly is the key. Here is a guiding principle that will help you to be consistent, and will help you to live in accordance with the law and the prophets. "Always treat others the way that you would like to be treated."

Sincerity and Your Heart

13-14 Accept my challenge to invite the Father into every area of your life.[14] A far better life is within your grasp, because you have heard my message. But there are very few people who will follow it. They are like those who enter by a narrow gate. Most people take the easy way—they enter through a wide gate. If you miss the narrow gate you will not be on the narrow road that leads to a better life. You will be on the wide road that leads to destruction.[15]

15 But even if you enter by the narrow gate you will still need to be careful. Watch out for false teachers. They are like wolves in sheep's clothing. You will be able to tell that they are false because their greed will show their true color. That will reveal what is in their hearts. 16 If you look at a piece of fruit you will know what kind of tree it came from. You do not pick grapes from a thorn bush, nor figs from a thistle bush. 17-20 Good fruit comes from good trees, and corrupt fruit comes from evil trees. Corrupt trees are worthless. They need to be chopped down and burned. False prophets' greed will show people the truth about their hearts. Get rid of them. Like bad apples, they are rotten to the core, and could spoil your whole crop if you spend any time with them.

21 You also need to watch out for people who falsely say that they have entered by the narrow gate. Not everyone who addresses me as "Lord" will enter the Kingdom of the "Heavens"—letting the Father guide every area of their life. Many such people seem to get it right on the outside but completely miss that their deceitful hearts are transparent to the world. They do not fool anyone but themselves. Their lives tell everyone exactly where their hearts are.

22 I know who is merely pretending to live from a pure heart. When judgment day comes many people will say to me that they were prophesying in my name, casting out demons in my name and were performing mighty miracles in my name. 23 But I will tell them, very plainly, that I never knew them and they must face judgment. They were devoted to themselves, hiding their selfish hearts behind the appearance of good behavior. They will not be able to hide on judgment day.

---

14. Jesus provided heart preparation for this teaching, earlier in the sermon, in the "False Righteousness" teaching, in chapter 6:1–6.

15. This passage is often thought of as a teaching about going to heaven or hell. It is significant to note that those words to not appear. The metaphor suggests that He is asking whether the listeners are really willing to take His teaching seriously. Staying on "the narrow road" is what leads to a far better life.

A TRANSFORMED HEART

24-27 Here is a closing picture for you. It is not enough if you just hear my words. You must put them into practice. When your life shows that you have heard my words, that will make you like a wise home builder. When my words direct your life, it will be like building your house on a rock. Your life will be solid. You will be able to withstand anything. The wind and the rain-swollen streams may beat upon your house but it will be as good as new. It has the right foundation. But if you hear my words and do not put them into practice, that will be like building your house on the sand. When the wind and the swollen streams pound against it, your house will be completely destroyed.

Now that we have come to the end of this sermon, we can see that "a better life" does not happen by finding ways to behave better. That would be another "rules approach" sermon, which is completely contrary to what this teaching is all about. Instead, we have heard Jesus encouraging us to make the Father our constant companion and to enjoy His friendship. He will assist us during our daily walk to grow richer and deeper, and to win strenuous heart battles so that we can live life from our heart and not from our hurt. Hearts that are properly prepared and attuned to His voice will allow Him to transform us into a certain kind of person—one whose life exudes forgiveness, genuineness, peacefulness and sincerity, and whose relationships naturally take on the qualities of love. When we invite the Father into our daily life and let Him guide us through a time of heart preparation, we are ready to live from a transformed heart. It happens from the inside out. This is putting His words into practice.

3

Translation Notes

APPROACHING *THE SERMON ON THE MOUNT*

You may wonder how I developed my understanding of *The Sermon on the Mount*, as presented in chapter 2. This sermon has held a certain fascination for me over the years, and there have been periods when I worked on it pretty extensively. During that study time it seemed like there was a long, arduous stairway still to climb, but each step of the ascension felt right. Perhaps the defining element has been that this approach to the sermon is truly life-changing. Jesus put it this way: "You don't pick figs from a thistle bush." A commercial put it this way: "Try it. You'll like it." Please let me tell you about a few of the crucial steps that have brought me up the stairway thus far.

1. *Taking another look at "The Beatitudes."* A high point of the year 1999 was to read *The Divine Conspiracy: Rediscovering our Hidden Life in God,* by Dallas Willard. One of the most unforgettable sections from that book is about *The Beatitudes* (chapter 4: Who is Really Well Off?—The Beatitudes). My heart leaped while I was reading that chapter, and I could not stop thinking how fundamental it is to approach *The Beatitudes* in this way.[1] I photocopied key pages from that chapter and faxed them off to friends, and I even bought extra copies of the book for my family because I had been so deeply affected by these profound ideas. What a relief it was for me to find that these difficult-to-understand verses actually lead to a far better life.

The point that Jesus was making in *The Beatitudes* is that the Father is available, no matter what. That is what *The Beatitudes* are about. It is not

---

1. Please refer to footnote 7 on page 9 for more of the specifics about this approach to *The Beatitudes*.

necessary, as I had previously been taught, to figure out the true meaning that is hidden within each *Beatitude,* in order to conclude that we should seek to be more spiritually broken, mournful, and the rest. That does not make sense, and I had sort of known that all along. If Jesus was divine, He should be able to explain things in a straight-forward fashion, not needing to keep the deeper meaning of His teaching obscure in any way. I always believed that *The Beatitudes* must be, somehow, easy to grasp. That is why Dr. Willard's approach was so refreshing to me. His door-opening ideas helped me a lot. It is *not* a good thing to be spiritually broken, as though that were something to strive for! Rather, it is a good thing to have the Father at our side because we are *already* spiritually broken. We don't have to stay that way when He assists us. In *The Beatitudes*, Jesus is not saying eight different things. He is emphasizing only one point—the Father's availability. That was His simple introduction to the sermon. Because the listeners understood it that way, they could hardly wait to hear what else He had to say. If He spoke so reassuringly about how God will be with them in the middle of their most unbearable suffering, then the rest of the sermon would certainly be worth hearing. If Jesus had breezed through eight major points, *The Beatitudes,* without developing them at all, His listeners' heads would have been spinning, and they would not have been in a frame of mind to catch the rest of the sermon. *The Beatitudes* are not eight points that need to be looked at separately. They are the development of one point—the Father's availability when we need Him most.

2. *Taking another look at "The Kingdom of the Heavens."* A second door-opener for me is how Dr. Willard explains "The Kingdom of the Heavens" (plural).[2] There is a completely different meaning in this phrase than in the mistranslated term, "The Kingdom of Heaven" (singular). The mistranslated term suggests that the kingdom is not a present reality, but it is something up in the sky, or it may be something that will someday be established here on earth. Jesus' message spread so quickly because those who heard Him speak about "the Father who is at your side," were blessed out of their socks. "The Kingdom of the Heavens" means that the Father is here among us, instead of somewhere far away.

Jesus was not trying to suggest that we should be planting His flag the whole world over, as though it were up to us to spread His kingdom. Instead, Jesus was saying that God's presence rules—He is already the

---

2. You may want to re-read the section from chapter 1 that begins on page 5.

King. His kingdom exists in power wherever you are. "The Kingdom of the Heavens" is an encouraging idea, letting the most deeply suffering people know that the Father is ready to help them anywhere in the world, any time, especially when everything is going wrong.

3. *Studying the sermon inductively.* In my seminary years I was taught the "inductive" Bible study method. It is so simple. You study each passage and each book of the Bible for what it says. You go over it and go over it until you can discover the words and ideas and phrases that elucidate the passage's deepest meaning. Only then can you let it penetrate your soul, and let it guide your heart.

Here is a key concept with inductive Bible study: It is a problem to try to compare and contrast all of the other instances where certain words and phrases appear throughout the Bible. What a distraction that can be. It is much more helpful to dive deeply into the text by using the inductive method. There is such a wealth of deeply satisfying material before you, that it behooves you to let it nourish you as completely as is possible.

Watch out for specialists, who smartly take you from context to context, and spin a web of Bible knowledge. How easy it is to *miss* that the Father wants to be your companion, whenever you get caught up in a maze of interesting biblical ideas. It's all about enjoying a relationship with the Father, and to look inductively at *The Sermon on the Mount* is to uncover that simple truth. He is available and wants to talk things over with you as they come up, so that you can turn every aspect of your life over to Him. You don't have to make it any more complicated than Jesus made it.

4. *Discovering the outline of the sermon.* As I continued to use the inductive method, I found that the whole sermon fits into an outline form, and I grew more confident that I was on the right track. Here is what makes sense to me: Jesus gave this sermon as a simply stated introduction to His teaching. There were no parables just yet. His listeners were beginners, and He knew that. They needed the uncomplicated ideas that would give them a good start.

> The Father is with you. You all have wounded hearts, and the Father will help you with the wounds. Just talk it all over with Him, and steadily follow His guidance. Carefully turn every area of your life over to Him. He will transform you into a person whose heart impels you to be forgiving, genuine, peaceful, sincere, and whose relationships naturally have the qualities of love.

The implications of taking that simple message seriously were life-changing back then, and they still are.

5. *Discovering that "The Lord's Prayer" is the sermon's climax.* About six years into my study of this sermon, I finally discovered that there are a few key words and ideas in *The Lord's Prayer* that are found throughout the rest of the sermon. Here is how I came to look at *The Lord's Prayer* differently, because of that discovery: In *The Lord's Prayer*, Jesus is telling us to talk about the sermon's main points with the Father.

About then I remembered another lesson from seminary, from Dr. Bailey, about how teachings were documented back then. Take the Apostle Peter's Pentecostal sermon in Acts, chapter 2, as an example. You can probably figure out that we do not have Peter's whole sermon written out, word for word. It would only be a three minute sermon if that were the case. I am sure that Peter delivered a longer speech than that. Would thousands of people change their lives after a speech that brief? Here's what makes more sense. The biblical account appears to be an outline of the ideas that he developed more completely, in the speech itself. Using the outline approach to document teachings like this one, we find that the main point is found in the center, and the supporting points are all mentioned both before and after the main point. What we have in Acts 2 is an outline with the main point in the center and the supporting points on each side, but there must have been many connecting ideas, introductory ideas, bridges between ideas, examples and comparisons, as well as comments about how to apply these ideas to the listeners' lives. We have the gist of Peter's sermon, but not a complete record.

I believe that this kind of documentation is what we have in *The Sermon on the Mount*. If Jesus spoke for a whole day, or for a few hours, we would expect that it would be recorded in this form. Considering that *The Beatitudes* are an introduction, the rest of Matthew's account lines up with the literary style mentioned by Dr. Bailey. We have *The Lord's Prayer* as the main point in the middle, and six supporting points mentioned both before and after it. If you accept that this literary approach is correct, then *The Lord's Prayer* must be the main point, and that is certainly the case. Talking everything over with the Father is what ties the whole sermon together. This sermon is not a collection of teachings. It is a coherent, simple sermon that listeners readily understood. By presenting his teaching in this commonly used style, the listeners could remember it when they got home, in the absence of sermon notes from handed-out programs.

One other factor needs to be included here. If you go through each of the separate teachings of *The Sermon on the Mount*, it is immediately clear that each is written in an abbreviated version. As was the case in Peter's sermon, we can be certain that there were introductory ideas for each point and connecting ideas between them. There were also tones of voice, gestures, and culturally-cued innuendoes that we cannot recover. Jesus must have been an absolutely fascinating teacher, and that suggests there must be a lot more that He must have included that day. Nonetheless, the outline that we have is phenomenal. The ideas are packed full of great power, even in their abbreviated form. However, without the connecting ideas and cultural cues being recorded, it is sometimes a stretch to know how Jesus tied His ideas together. It takes some work to put the trees together in a way that show us the forest. Assuming that the teachings were not presented randomly, and assuming that the outline form mentioned above fits the sermon, we can more correctly tell how some of the ideas are linked. The often-quoted teaching on "being perfect" is a good example.

6. *Finding a more suitable approach to the "be perfect" teaching.* "Be perfect, just like the Father in heaven." How can He just say that? It makes sense to view this teaching not as a separate teaching, but it is a part of the "retaliation" section. I always found it rather quizzical that Jesus would have told people to be perfect if He did not mean it. How could it make sense to believe that Jesus was telling us to strive for perfection? I had to ask myself why He would put such a teaching right there in the sermon. No matter how that was explained, it never made sense to me. It makes more sense when we find it under the "retaliation" heading.

A few years ago I was leading a Sunday School class about the teachings of Jesus. I often relied on F. F. Bruce's book, *The Hard Sayings of Jesus*, as a resource in developing the lessons. When I came to the "be perfect" teaching, Dr. Bruce's book helped a lot. He places it in the context of, "so you want to be sons of the Father? Here is what that will look like."

> "Your Father . . . makes his sun rise on the evil and on the good, and sends rain on the just and on the unjust" (Matt. 5:45). He bestows his blessings without discrimination. [My note: In that parched land, the rain was as much a blessing as was the sun, so this teaching said that the Father sends life-giving blessings to everyone.] The followers of Jesus are children of God, and they

should manifest the family likeness by doing good to all, even to those who deserve the opposite. So, said Jesus, go the whole way in doing good, just as God does (page 75).

Dr. Bruce also helps us to figure out why the word "perfect" makes its way into the text. We come up with "perfect" by looking at the Greek word used there. It helps to keep in mind that Jesus delivered this sermon in the language spoken by the people—Aramaic. "We do not know the precise Aramaic words that Jesus used on this occasion, but they probably meant, 'You must be perfect (that is, all-embracing, without any restriction) in your acts of mercy or kindness, for that is what God is like'" (page 76).

Now it all makes sense. Jesus was speaking about how very hard it is to stop the automatic, human propensity to retaliate. Loving enemies is not a natural reaction. It takes a transformed heart. Jesus strongly identifies *treating everyone with mercy and kindness*, as a trait that shows whose family a person belongs to. Being perfect means loving without discrimination, which is precisely what shows up in God's family. That is not a teaching which is hard to understand. Dr. Bruce says that it is hard to obey. I would add that without a transformed heart, it will not be possible to treat everyone with mercy and kindness. However, a God-directed heart will not retaliate. Instead, it will deliver kindness to everyone, because that is the way the Father is. The way people treat enemies reveals their true family likeness.

7. *Discovering that the "salt of the earth" teaching is about hopelessness.* One other finding that comes from the outline approach needs to be included here, because it shows how the outline approach helps us recognize the progression between thoughts. Take a look at the "salt and light" teaching. The outline suggests that this will be where we find His first teaching about the heart's wounds, immediately following the introduction, and that turns out to be the case. Jesus is not saying, in this often-quoted teaching, that it is great to know that we are like salt. He is saying that we can feel hopeless, like the salt that is thrown away on the ground, when we fail, time after time, and completely feel useless, just like an old discarded pile of salt.

When giving an illustration or a parable, teachers like Jesus were asking listeners to identify with the story's main character. You can see why, when Jesus was asked by a legal expert, "Who is my neighbor," He gave the parable of the Good Samaritan. As that parable developed, Jesus made the expert feel pretty uncomfortable. First there was a Priest and then a Levite who passed by the traveler near death, and neither helped. These were characters with whom the legal expert could identify, and in the parable they were completely without compassion. Then along comes a person whom the legal expert despises—a Samaritan—and he has an unbelievable degree of compassion. The story left the expert in an unmanageable position. He could not identify with the compassionate character in the story. That is the way parables worked. The listener identified with something in the story, and Jesus made an unforgettable point.

So now we can examine Jesus' teaching about salt and light, and begin by asking ourselves what the listener is supposed to identify with. Jesus starts out by telling them exactly what to identify with. "You are the salt on the ground." Okay. Now what does He have to say about salt on the ground? It can easily become tainted and useless. They all knew that this happened often enough. Their salt usually came from scrapings along the edge of the Dead Sea. If it was impure, it was eternally useless. That is certainly an illustration dealing with a very disturbing heart wound—hopelessness. If you are salt thrown away, lying uselessly on the ground, you must believe there is no hope for you. There *is* no hope for this kind of salt, and Jesus' listeners realized that He knew how hopeless they can feel. Then Jesus followed that picture with a hope-filled illustration. "You are the light that shines throughout the world. When you follow your calling as light, you will change the world. You do not need to remain hopeless."

It makes sense to me that Jesus' first target for helping people with wounded hearts, would be hopelessness. For more than a quarter of a century I have been listening to what's going on in wounded hearts, and I have learned that the darkest wound is hopelessness. After all, if hopelessness is present, the person has no reason to work on it—that would be useless too, because *nothing in the world can help.* That is where Jesus comes in, because He can offer healing, cleansing and truth, and these will take the "less" out of "hopeless."

8. *This sermon appears at the very start of Jesus' career as a rabbi, so we need to keep it in that context.* When many pastors look at this sermon, they take a traditional approach. The sermon has long been viewed as a collection of Jesus' sayings, so each teaching can be taken as a separate sermon topic. Since each teaching is ripe with meaning, pastors tend to get caught up in each one. There is plenty of rich material to draw from.

They usually do a fine job understanding each tree but can miss the forest. Here is the forest that I see. The story of Jesus' early ministry, as *Matthew* presents it, is not far enough along for Jesus to preach a complicated sermon, at the time He gave *The Sermon on the Mount*. His message was directed to first timers. These people needed to hear a "starter" sermon, one that encouraged them to get God into their lives. The more complicated topics came later, through parables, some of which are explained in detail, a little later in the *Gospel According to Matthew*. What I find striking about this sermon is its simplicity. As Dr. Bruce put it, the teaching is not hard to understand. It is hard to obey.

9. *I overcame my hesitation to think in non-traditional ways.* The teachings of Jesus can be likened to a swimming pool that is shallow enough for small children to wade in and deep enough for elephants to swim in. There is a lot of room to swim out there in the deep end. Don't be afraid of diving deeply into new areas. Don't be afraid of trying new swimming strokes. If you are working out, try swimming in a different lane.

Here is what I am trying to convey in this closing thought. I have heard many very good, blessed-by-God sermons taken from *The Sermon on the Mount,* and God has reached me while listening to them, even if the speaker did not see the same thing in the text that I see. God has helped me change my life because I listened to His message that came to me from an unexpected source. It is not up to me to tell God how to reach people, by using a particular approach to this sermon. He can bless people very easily, because His teachings are many-faceted, overflowing with meaning, and His Spirit comes into hearts that welcome Him. I offer this approach to *The Sermon on the Mount* as another lane in the swimming pool. It gives me goose bumps to think that people may get closer to God because He reaches them when they swim in this lane. You will do yourself no earthly good if you stay comfortable, lying upon the pool deck. He can hardly wait to help you live a far better life, by overcoming hopelessness, treating everyone with generosity and talking everything over with Him. Get in and swim.

An Interlude

A FEW YEARS AGO, my wife and I went on a ranger-led horseback excursion high up in the High Sierra Nevadas. The horses were corralled not far from some redwood groves, but the ride began in a forest of pine trees and cedars. We rode single file along a shaded trail, with about 15 other riders, and had no thoughts about the nearby redwood trees.

I am not accustomed to horseback riding, so I concentrated mostly on watching the ground in front of my horse. I suppose it was a nice little ride for my wife and for the other horse lovers, but for me it was pretty dusty and uneventful. There was no announcer telling me what I was passing. There was no printed trail guide to describe the surrounding flora and fauna, as we slowly made our way along the narrow trail. We did not stop at Starbucks to chat about the squirrels and the blue jays who were scolding us so profusely. We didn't even have any handy little plastic containers of water.

Well into the trip, the trail rounded a bend, and the greenish-grey trees with three foot trunks suddenly gave way to majestic redwoods, whose trunks were at least fifteen feet wide. The late afternoon sunlight was spotlighting the giant trunks on the gently rising slope, just off to the left, illuminating their reddish bark and drawing our attention to the velvet texture. For those trees beyond the thousand year mark, the lower branches have been missing for centuries. That left absolutely nothing between our eyes and the sheer beauty of the tree trunks, which must have been at least one hundred feet tall before there were any branches. That is a span about two freeway lanes wide, and more than seven stories high. "Eye-catching" is an understatement. "Heart-stopping" is an understatement. The trees seemed way too big. We all were unprepared.

The horses were not impressed. For them it was nothing more than another afternoon of walking along through the forest. But I wanted to dismount and drink it all in. Those trees would not be ignored. "How awesome!" For the first time that afternoon, the riders raised their voices in cackling excitement to one another. It was such a wonderful surprise that we could not keep our amazement all bottled up inside. So what if we had seen redwood trees a hundred times? When they present themselves in the afternoon sun, it is like seeing redwoods for the first time.

Maybe you have read *The Sermon on the Mount* many times, and have heard a hundred preachers talk about it. It can still knock you off your horse.

Part Two

Living

4

Christian Counseling

THERE IS AN URGE within each of us to live a better life. It is not optional, it will not just, somehow, eventually go away, and it will not stay quiet for very long. People are impelled to search until they find it.

Having reviewed Jesus' most comprehensive teaching, we can see that He presented, in a simple fashion, what it will take to satisfy that search. Christian Counseling needs to be on the same page with Jesus here. It almost goes without saying that Jesus' teaching is supposed to be where Christians seek direction for practically any topic. But particularly when the topic is helping people live a better life, Christian Counseling needs to work very hard to be entirely consistent with His teaching.

> Whatever Jesus taught about reaching a better life needs to be the core, the essence, the heart of Christian Counseling. If there are to be "approaches" to Christian Counseling, they need to be footnotes to His teaching.

A BRIEF SUMMARY OF JESUS' TEACHING ABOUT LIVING A BETTER LIFE

People are Broken, and Need God's Guidance

There is an unseen reality that supplies immense power to deal with the brokenness that haunts us all.[1] It is the spiritual realm. The reality that each of us sees with our eyes is not the reality that is eternal. Human beings need God's help to enter the eternal reality or they will not reach

---

1. This initial idea is based on *The Beatitudes* and *The Lord's Prayer*, in *Matthew* 5:3–12 and 6:7–13. It is supported by Malony and Augsburger in their recently released *Introduction to Christian Counseling.* "Increasing and maintaining a sense of God is, indeed, the master motive for Christian counselors" (pages 28–30).

a fulfilling end to their search for a better life. When they acknowledge their spiritual need for the Father and welcome Him into their daily walk, He will become their companion and will provide steady guidance to transform their lives. Everything else about reaching a better life depends upon this first step. This is where the spiritual power of God is welcomed into a life that would otherwise be headed toward misery. No matter how deep the struggle, Jesus teaches that the Father's guidance will be available when we need it most. A remarkable joy comes from being close to Him, and it provides a tremendous boost, especially during times of trial. Count on Him. He will always be available.

Wounded Hearts Need God's Healing

The heart is where God connects to people.[2] It is where He makes His guidance from the spiritual realm available for every daily decision, every trial and every conflict. When a heart is wounded, it is seriously blocked from receiving God's input. Jesus mentioned six areas where healing for wounded hearts is needed—hopelessness, contempt, lust, dishonesty, retaliation and false righteousness. Healing in these areas prepares hearts for the Father's guidance.

The Father's Companionship Helps People to Live from Transformed Hearts

God's constant availability to work in a transformed heart will make it possible to live from the heart, so that life will flow "from the inside out."[3] His guidance will show up in particular ways—ways that indicate He is leading. Over time, a certain kind of person will emerge—one who exudes forgiveness, genuineness, peacefulness and sincerity, and whose relationships naturally take on the qualities of love. Keeping a heart free from wounds and talking everything over with the Father will produce enough strength to withstand any storm. A far better life is reachable.

---

2. This second idea is based on problems highlighted in the "Preparing Your Heart" teaching of *The Sermon on the Mount*, in *Matthew* 5:13—6:6.

3. This third idea is based on the "Transformed Heart" teaching in *The Sermon on the Mount*, in *Matthew* chapter 6:14—7:27.

AN APPROACH TO CHRISTIAN COUNSELING: LIVING FROM A TRANSFORMED HEART

When I let the ideas from this sermon sink into my mind, I find myself with a heightened sense of awareness. There is a unique, compelling draw to read through it again and think about it, and later I have to go back and read it again from the start. It helps me to write out the ideas that come to me, and then re-write them a few times. Often the ideas hit me in new ways after a few days, and I end up re-writing everything. This would be hard work, if it were not so energizing. At times like that, I know that God has let me come close to a great river of truth, and I believe that I sort of "get it." Here is what is so energizing—that this great river of truth is *available* to me. The Father *wants me* to "get it," and is taking His time with me so that I can get a bigger dose of His great truth. And even then, when I come to the same part of the sermon a few months later, I "get a little more" from the text and I am energized anew.

That is the way Jesus' teaching is. It keeps calling to you in a most appealing way, and you want to go back and visit it all over again. As was mentioned in the previous chapter, His teaching has been likened to a swimming pool that is shallow enough for small children to wade in and deep enough for elephants to swim in. That picture makes sense to me. There is a lot of room out there in the deep end, and we all owe it to ourselves to dive in and swim for a while.

By now I have outlined what I see in Jesus' teaching, particularly about how life can be transformed by the Father's presence. Next I want to detail out how this material can be the basis for Christian Counseling. This approach is my "footnote" to His teaching, based on the summary outlined above. Here are the three areas that make sense to me on which to base Christian Counseling. Please dive in with me for a swim.

God's Involvement, at Every Point, is Essential

I absolutely love what our pastor told us about his prayer life during a recent sermon.[4] He shared in a very helpful, personally disclosing way what happens when he gets alone with God. As he described it, he goes downstairs early in the morning and talks things over with the Father. He protects this alone time with God, so it will not get overlooked. Here is

---

4. This first idea is based on *The Beatitudes* and *The Lord's Prayer*, in *Matthew* chapter 5:3–12 and 6:7–13.

what I find wonderful—he said that he never knows ahead of time just what God will want to talk about with him. Sometimes it is praying for certain people, sometimes it has to do with new ideas coming to him from the Word of God, sometimes it is about developments in our church, or there may be something taking place in his family that he needs to talk over with God, but he emphasized that he has no idea just what will come up until he shows up.

As our pastor was sharing this, I was furiously jotting down a few notes to myself about how this is exactly what it is like for me at the beginning of each counseling session. I was so excited about what I was hearing that I could not keep quiet. I started to whisper something to my wife but she was more interested in listening to the pastor. Here is why I was so affirmed by what he was saying—it seems that he and I invite God into our days in pretty much the same way.

When a session in my office gets started we usually pray for a short while. I often begin by thanking God for His goodness, welcoming Him into our time together, asking Him to fill us with His Spirit, to pour out His blessing onto us, to guide us into any area of discussion that will be helpful, and to protect us from evil. There are, of course, plenty of variations. One person added a prayer about letting more of God flow through him "unhindered." That is what he was led to pray right then. Sometimes it seems important to ask for relief from suffering, or about healing for a wound that has been exposed, or about the person's family life, but my first goal is to empty myself so that I will not carry out the session under my own direction. The other person or people in the room may want to pray as well, but there is no formula for the prayer time. We ask God to lead, first and foremost. As our pastor put it, I never know what is going to come up until I show up.

Relationships with God need to make room for His input, especially during prayers.[5] As a session goes forward there may be times when we spontaneously find a reason to pray, if it seems we are being led. Sometimes scriptures may come to mind, and we may quote them or turn to the Word to read a few verses. When we come to the meeting's end we usually close with a prayer of healing and protection, or we may sense that more prayer will be needed so that the healing can continue. At times like that we may find it necessary to extend the session. As we

---

5. *Hearing God*, by Dallas Willard, can be considered to be a trustworthy trail guide for following His guidance.

begin we do not know what direction God may take us, and later we do not know how to bring it to a close until we get there. There is a sense of letting it happen, as opposed to making it happen. Even when certain issues or feelings are urgently waiting to be discussed, it can be crucial to stop everything and invite God to take over. There are no bells or whistles, and there is not usually a dramatic Word from God. We just talk things over with each other and Him, do what we can to move ahead through the painful material that comes up, and seek His healing for any wounds that become exposed. Most of the time it is a relief, and often there is a particular God-given joy. That joy is distinctive. It has His blessing, which makes it much richer than "relief."

We do our best to rely on His guidance not only for the content of a session, but also for the process as God shapes it. For example, a husband may unexpectedly show up, or unexpectedly not show up, a pastor may decide at the last minute to join us, or sometimes a friend who has come along should be brought with us into the office for on-the-spot prayer backup. Sometimes the extra person will be needed to pray for us in the waiting room during a session. God has something for each person to contribute, which makes it important, as the session moves along, to pay attention to His guidance.

Then there is the problem of arriving late, arriving very late, or being unable to attend because of a last-minute situation. Here is what makes sense to me. I tell the person who is calling because they are stuck on the freeway, or are calling in a late cancellation, something like this. "God must have something else in mind for you right now." When we begin the re-scheduled meeting on another day, I often say something like, "God must have something particular in mind for you *right now*, because He has had to work pretty hard to get us here at *this* time!" The bottom line is this. Every person who shows up is needed to contribute something in particular, and will receive something in particular. Whatever amount of time we have is enough time for God to give us what He has for us. When there is a cancel and I have some extra time on my hands, God must have something else for *me* right then. God is with us, no matter how unexpected the circumstances, and He wants to give us something really beneficial. It helps to expect that He is providing the right setting, even if it seems contrary to our planning.

Following our pastor's sermon about prayer, as we were driving home, I took the opportunity to talk about all of this with my wife. After

I mentioned to her how I keep asking for God's guidance as a session moves along, and how we seldom know before hand just which direction we will go, she said, "Well, maybe that's why people get better." Of course, she was correct. We invite Him to take us in the right direction, and He provides healing when we get there.

One person told me that she had been working with other Christian counselors for many years, and that I am the first one to pray with her. I tried not to act too surprised or disappointed, but I must say that it makes me more than a little sad to hear about other Christian counselors who do not include a time of prayer. After all, isn't it God's guidance and healing that makes the counseling *Christian* in the first place?

It seems to me that prayer is central to the Christian life, and to christian counseling. Each day can start out on the right path when we open up to God for His direction. When we make plans apart from Him we should not expect the best. The same can be said about a counseling session. God wants to be involved in every area of our lives. Particularly when it comes to the sensitive areas that come up in counseling, He definitely is eager to pour out His blessing if He is invited.

The Beatitudes and *The Lord's Prayer* are the introduction and the climax of *The Sermon on the Mount*, and this is how I read them—the Father will be with you no matter how seriously broken you are, so keep talking everything over with Him. If you want to live a better life, this is where you start and this is where you stay—welcoming Him into your life and talking everything over with Him as it comes up, even in the worst of circumstances. For me, this is the foundation of my work as a Christian Counselor. I deeply believe that it is essential to keep an open line to Him each time we work with wounded hearts. He has consistently shown that He will provide answers, and many times those answers leave us strengthened by a sense of great joy. His presence has that effect, just as He taught.

It is God's active involvement that makes life work, and that is also the case when it comes to counseling sessions. Being attuned to His guidance can provide encouraging progress in helping wounded hearts.

God Wants to Provide Healing for Wounded Hearts

Despite Jesus' teaching that people who believe in Him would do "even greater works" than His (*John* 14:12) and despite two thousand years of people praying for family and friends whenever they are afflicted, I often find an unexpected reluctance among Christians about "praying for healing."[6] Even using the word "healing" can invite a sort of scientific enquiry about what I really mean. It seems to me that prayer for God's healing is the obvious course of action whenever pain comes up, so I must believe that Christian counselors who do not yet include healing prayer will begin to use it after they re-visit Jesus' teachings.[7]

There is a whole shelf full of books that tell us about healing prayer, and how it pertains to Christian counseling. Among my favorites are books from Neil Anderson, Rita Bennett, Charles Kraft, Leanne Payne and Pamela Perez.[8] These authors and others attest to the fact that the time-honored tradition of praying for people works very well for many aspects of counseling.

A few years ago I worked together with four Christian counselors and put together a book which can be included above on the list of books about healing. We decided to put this title on it—*The Life Model: Living from the Heart Jesus Gave You.* I feel incredibly blessed to have worked with those gifted counselors. They brought new areas of knowledge to me that I would otherwise have missed. You may want to pick up that book and look over the chapters on "Maturity" and "Belonging," which those counselors helped me to learn about. In a nutshell, that book highlights certain areas which can prevent us from "living from our heart." Problems with maturity, belonging and trauma recovery can block us at the heart level, and the book opens up pathways to get through those blockages. *The Life Model* points out areas for "heart work" which involve prayerful healing. There is no separate chapter on prayer, *per se*, but healing prayer is included throughout the book.

Most of my work in recent years has been devoted to helping people receive healing for traumas, but it has not always been that way. About three years after I had gained my state license I was forced to reach a

---

6. This second idea is based on problems highlighted in the "Preparing Your Heart" teaching of *The Sermon on the Mount*, in *Matthew* chapter 5:13—6:6.

7. Even though the word "healing" does not appear in *The Lord's Prayer,* asking Him to forgive our offenses, to help us with temptation and to deliver us from evil are often included in healing prayers. Perhaps the central idea in *The Lord's Prayer* is inviting Him to control everything in our life, as He controls heaven. It seems pretty clear that seeking His healing for pain is going to happen while we are allowing Him to take full control.

8. Some titles by these authors are listed in the Reference section.

sobering conclusion. I had read that clients with deep wounds will "improve" if they stay in therapy. For about a year and a half I was working with some deeply wounded persons. I had been giving it my best effort, which meant a lot of reading and consulting with fellow counselors, so that I could be more effective with these folks. I eventually came to the point where I realized that they were not getting better. In some cases they were getting much worse.

It was time to learn more about helping these precious, suffering people. I needed to look for training in the Christian aspects of counseling. I had already completed a few years of training in the psychological domain, and now it was time for me to receive some training in the spiritual area. The psychological material by itself was proving to be insufficient. One of the counselors in our center had been praying with her clients for the healing of memories, and had quite a lot of experience in the spiritual arena. When I spoke with her we decided to set aside two hours each Monday afternoon to work together. She brought along her prayer partner, who had a remarkable gift in the area of spiritual discernment, and they included me in the prayer counseling. Each week we made plans to work together with one of her clients or one of mine on Monday afternoons. The three of us would invite the clients' prayer partners, marriage partners, pastors or friends to come along and join us as we prayed.

Please try to keep in mind that I had received my clinical training in *scientifically oriented* settings, and had obtained my license as a psychologist to use interventions that did not involve spirituality. I was a counselor who was a Christian, but there was nothing distinctively Christian about my counseling. There had already been about 10 years between the beginning of my graduate training in psychology and the beginning of my spiritual training. During that time I had learned a lot, but I soon found out that there was a whole new realm to delve into. Over the following two years, as my spiritual training took shape, I was challenged like never before. Here are the main lessons from that time.

1. *Wounds are physical and they are spiritual.* People's suffering is incredibly deep, but they will open up about it if you give them a chance. They will get right into their most painful material, which will always have a spiritual side to it.

2. *Spiritual attacks are to be expected whenever the pain is exposed.* The enemy's lies are about never getting better, not being good enough or

being fatally flawed, or there may be some other spiritual stronghold that needs a prayerful time of "working through," in order to break the lies.

3. *Beware of quick fixes.* Deep suffering opens up over a long period of time, and we need God's patience while attending to it, until it is properly relieved. Too often, the immediate relief of some pain feels so wonderfully "blessed by God," that a person will hope everything is suddenly okay. "I'm done. God is done, and I'm doing great!" It makes more sense to persist in seeking His guidance for as long as healing of particular wounds is still underway.

4. *Spiritual attacks should be expected.* Counselors' every fear, weakness, conflict and character flaw will be targeted by Satan. He does not want this work to succeed. Those on the front lines will take personal hits, and so will their families. This is not intended for beginners, nor for the faint of heart. A strong faith, along with two years of steady training and prayer support is a minimum. As Paul put it, we are afflicted in every way but not crushed, perplexed but not driven to despair, persecuted but not forsaken, struck down but not destroyed (2 Corinthians 4:8–9). Those who persist are those who depend on the Father's companionship while the battle is being fought. As each battle comes to an end, we find that God has been steadily at work, bringing good out of it.

5. *Ask God to help you to grow in the area of discernment.* We each need to learn to recognize Satan's interference as it comes against us, and to rely on the power of God. Remember that when Jesus sent out His disciples He mentioned that they would face demons, so we should not be surprised to find ourselves in spiritual battles. There is no splendor, nor anything to brag about when it comes to winning spiritual battles. It is ugly and the only good part is when the present battle is over. A seasoned warrior waits for orders, knows where the power comes from and uses it wisely. The battle is the Lord's.

6. *Learn to trust God's faithfulness.* When two or more are gathered for prayer, God is in their midst. He will not only show up, but He will deliver from evil and will often provide an inspiring sense of joy as the session closes.[9]

7. *Spiritual lessons apply everywhere.* God also wants to pour out His blessing at times other than scheduled prayer sessions. His intention

---

9. Joy is not promised, nor is it the goal. Disclaimers aside, God is faithful, and He supplies healing for wounded hearts in grand and in subtle ways.

is to do this kind of work during every hour of the day, in and out of the office.

Now that I am a few years down the road since my initial spiritual training, I have met people of all sorts who are involved in the psychological-spiritual counseling field. It is easy to see that each counselor has a slant on how to properly attend to hurting people. I must admit that we all bring our own perspective along with us, and we tend to overrate our own ideas.

That being said, over time I have come to value the leaders in this field who never lose their quest for learning from both the psychological and the spiritual realms. I worry about "approaches" that are strictly one or the other, and I really worry about leaders in counseling who over-promote their own method, and quit being devoted to learning. There continue to be important discoveries in developmental, neurological and clinical psychology, and in trauma recovery, so continuing education is essential. "Education" is not exactly what is needed in the spiritual realm, although disciplined study helps. I am inclined to trust people whose spiritual walk impels them to be unsatisfied with the *status quo*. God wants to move us into a deeper, richer life with Him, so that should always be our direction. People on a quest to do better in both areas deserve the most trust. They tend to refrain from promoting their work, and still lead productive lives.

In order to be a part of God's work in healing wounded hearts, some serious training is needed. We need a thorough understanding of what psychology has to teach us, and we need to be growing in responsiveness to the Father's guidance. What I have found is that most of my work seems to center around Jesus' concerns, namely, that hearts need to receive healing for the wounds that produce hopelessness, contempt, lust, dishonesty, retaliation and false righteousness. That is why I spend most of my time helping people seeking His healing for those traumas. That approach helps people live from their heart instead of living from their hurt.

Living from a Transformed Heart

As was mentioned near the beginning of this chapter, in the brief summary of Jesus' teaching, living from a transformed heart gradually causes a certain kind of character to emerge.[10] The person begins to automati-

---

10. This third idea is based on the "Living from a Transformed Heart" teaching in *The Sermon on the Mount*, in *Matthew*, chapter 6:14—7:27.

cally show forgiveness, genuineness, peacefulness and sincerity, and enjoys relationships that naturally take on the qualities of love. That happens from the inside out, because the person has been close to the Father. A companionship has developed, and He loves the closeness, just as we do. The pleasure goes both ways.

I have noticed something that happens when we draw closer to the Father. We begin to change the world. Jesus mentioned this just after *The Beatitudes*. People's lives around us are affected in positive ways. As we open up to His goodness, we begin to glow like never before, and our joy is contagious. Our actions flow from His goodness that wells up within us, and the way we relate to the people around us points to the Father as the source of those actions. When we see the Father using us to bring His goodness into the lives of others, we move as close to Him as we can get. His likeness begins to emerge, which is the source of the forgiveness, genuineness and the rest of the characteristics that are evident when we live from a transformed heart.

I have met people, from time to time, who have described moments in their lives when they were unexpectedly filled with a special kind of joy while their actions were being directed by God—living from their hearts. Here is one such account that I received from a friend. It came up during a conversation, and I asked Michelle to write down her thoughts for me, so I could share them here.

> When I was in high school I saw the movie, *Chariots of Fire*, for the first time. I have never forgotten the words of the famous Olympian sprinter in that movie who said, "When I run, I feel God's pleasure." He was a missionary to China, and his ministry there was on hold while he trained for the Olympics. The movie showed him with an incredible smile on his face, whenever he was running. God's pleasure was all over him! Since that time I have claimed a similar truth as my own, stating that "when I *sing* I feel God's pleasure."

> I have loved music ever since I was a little girl. Musical ventures, from singing to playing the piano to dramatic musical endeavors, have been important throughout this season in my life. Yet recently I have noticed that something is beginning to change me at my deepest core, with regard to music.

> I have been leading worship in my church once a month now for the past six months, and I have begun to notice that a profoundly deep spiritual stirring has been taking place inside of me, in a dif-

ferent way than ever before. I have had an awakening to God's holiness, intertwined with a keen sense of the power of the relationship between a life that is daily spent in worship, and that of being involved in leading others in worship. I have become increasingly aware that I want to live every moment of every day in complete surrender to Jesus, which is leading me to be drawn into a newfound love relationship with Him that is truly vibrant and authentic. Consequently, I am noticing that I am actually feeling God's pleasure as I respond emotionally to Him, which translates to a longing to harmonize with God's Spirit in such a way that His anointing flows continually, whether I am leading worship or I am out running errands. I am not performing when I lead the congregation in turning their focus to the Lord; instead, I am fully worshipping, while inviting others to join me in doing the same. I am humbled, and in awe as I see people responding emotionally to God, sensing His presence in the room. It is here that I Timothy 6:19 becomes a reality for me, as I "take hold of the life that is truly life!"

Confirmation of the work of God's Spirit took place recently as a woman in my church sent me a bouquet of flowers, with an attached note that read:

"For the many gifts you give to the Body of Christ
For your beautiful voice that allows us to enter into His Gates with
    Praise
For all the love you model so well, that when I watch you I see
    JESUS

I am so glad that you are my friend and I celebrate you . . . ."

Words cannot express the joy I felt as I read these words because they reflected that she sees Jesus alive in me. Now I have a deeper understanding of what it means to say, "When I worship I feel God's pleasure."

These showers of joy from God are life-changing. Afterwards, we look back on them as pillars of our faith, and our confidence in God continues to grow. When looking for an answer to the question, "How can I get that kind of joy?" I would suggest that it is better if you don't *try* to get it. Instead, make it a habit to praise God regularly, to keep seeking healing for your wounded heart, and to keep on letting His words direct your life. *This is living in the Kingdom of the Heavens.* Before long you will find yourself doing His work, and He will shower His joy upon you when you least expect it.

A church can provide just the right opportunities for becoming a part of God's work. When a church operates as it should many people get involved, working together. Group efforts abound. In cases where a large group of people are working together and are overflowing from the goodness that God has placed in each of their hearts, something happens that is certainly noticeable, yet hard to describe. "Euphoria" is one word. The feeling is joy, "to the max." It is infectious, and everybody can tell that something supernatural is happening. Some people identify it as the presence of the Holy Spirit, and that may be exactly what it is. I believe it comes from God's pleasure. He feels better about a few people doing His work together because they are devoted to Him, than He does about 100,000 people watching a sporting event. He blesses their efforts and sends a shower of joy. People who get caught up in the joy are amazed. They get blessed, and they are not even sure exactly what happened.

There is something important to emphasize here, that cannot be left as an afterthought. Get involved. Do you want to know what it is like to live in the Kingdom of the Heavens? Think about it, talk about it and then make it happen. Do it. You cannot observe it. You have to *be* a part of what God is doing in the world in order to receive a shower of joy from Him. There are thinkers, there are talkers and there are people who make it happen. Make it happen. There is learning and there is living. Live it. Jesus said it this way in the fitting conclusion to His sermon: *It is not enough if you just hear my words. You must put them into practice* (Matthew 7:24).

Here is how one church encourages people to "make it happen." This is a church that is boosted by the power generated from home groups. A very important part of the home group program is getting people involved in the activities of the church. Very clearly, it is emphasized that each person who comes into a home group is urged—practically required—to get involved in some way, serving in at least one of the church-directed programs. If a new person in a home group cannot find any particular program to plug into, they are pointed towards the children's ministry. There are always people needed to help with the very active children's ministry. Contributing to on-going group efforts is how that church supports people's growth. They feel God's pleasure as they see that they are being used to enrich the lives of children and families. God is at work and they are a part of it.

Julianne is one person who has gotten involved in God's work at that church. About six years ago she rededicated her life to God and became fully involved in spiritual growth. She joined the choir and was deeply blessed by God's goodness there, time after time. She is a person who grasps how important it is to make things happen. Julianne heard God's call, put it into practice, and she has been steadily seeking to grow closer to God. Not only has she been singing in the choir, she has gotten into a home group and pitched into the on-going church life in many ways. From helping with four-year-olds, to contributing countless hours to special events for kids and adults, she has let God open quite a few service doors for her. One night she had a shower of joy that she could not keep to herself—it was just too sweet for her to stay quiet about. With a bounce in her step and a sparkle in her eyes she began to put words to this remarkable experience.

God had placed her to help with the Jr. High youth group. Mind you, this is a big group, with 200 or more young people in attendance at most events. She became a small group leader for a few of the girls, and tried to find places where she was needed. At a big, rowdy Jr. High event one night she was placed behind the one-way windows, looking out over the large auditorium. All of the young people's activities were taking place on the other side of those windows. This room is used on Sundays by nursing mothers during the worship services. But that night Julianne was placed there all alone, to pray for the young people as the meeting unfolded in front of her. I suppose it was a little like seeing what angels see, quietly attuning herself to God and watching Him work as He was moving in the hearts of those young people. She knew many of the kids out there, and she could see them thoroughly involved in their rambunctious activities, behaving exactly like Jr. High youngsters.

Her prayer time began by singing a few praise songs, and soon she found God coming alive in her. Shortly, she began to sing songs that she was creating as she went along, and she did not even keep track of what she was singing. God's goodness was overflowing in her and His closeness was the power that directed her prayers. Weeping, she began to pray for the young people she could see before her in the auditorium, and soon she was overtaken by a wave of God's spirit. She wrote me a brief note, about what happened that evening.

I still cannot get it out of my mind or heart. God's presence in that room was so tangible I couldn't even sit in the chair. I ended up with my face in the carpet—scared to death to raise my head. Maybe "scared" isn't the right word. It wasn't like I was frightened. It was every cell in my body more alive than it had ever been, more sensitive to the air. It was *the created* in the hand of *the Creator*, unable to do anything but worship. I almost feel odd relating this story as it was the most intimate experience of my life. The presence of God was there alone for me. He knew my name. He knew my life—the beginning, the end and everything in between. Yet in reality, none of that mattered. All that I could "see" was the pure love and awesome, glorious power of the One who holds my very existence in His Hand.

One boy in particular came to dwell in her prayers, and she did not even know his name. She already had a hunch that his life was in trouble, so her conscious prayers for him had some direction. She had seen that his behavior was pretty far out of control just before she had begun to pray, and there was a concern that the leaders may need to expel him from the group activity that evening. Still, her prayers for him sort of took off on their own, and she sensed God's pleasure as she held this young man up in prayer.

When I emerged from the nursing mothers' room the first thing that I saw was the boy, surrounded by college interns, laughing and bonding and sharing God's love with this poor kid. It was God's true family at work in a fallen world—reaching out, loving the unlovable, being vessels of His power, living in His glory.

Julianne added that God had done something miraculous that evening in the group she was praying for, and in the life of that boy. She knew that God had warmed up his heart that evening, while she was praying. This confirmed to her that the work God was carrying out in and through her, was His work. No wonder every cell in her body was more alive than ever. It was Him drawing her close, and she was ready to respond from her heart.

As Julianne first recounted this to me she was caught up being exuberant about what it was like to be drenched in a shower of joy from God. She said that she could now tell me with conviction, that there is a universal battle going on all of the time—in people's minds, in the songs we sing and in the air itself.

Jesus was right—God's presence in the air around us, in the Kingdom of the Heavens, is a power that we must stay in touch with. The universal battle will devour us if we ignore God's power that is so readily available. When she became aligned with it, Julianne's soul joined in the battle, and she became a part of the victory celebration that is taking place outside of our physical realm. (These are mostly her words and phrases.)

That is the way God works. As we enter into the Kingdom of the Heavens He fills us up on a regular basis. When we learn to open up to Him more and more, He uses us to do His work in increasingly wonderful ways. Julianne lets God move her, and she responds by getting involved in His work. She is careful to add that ups-and-downs have pock-marked her life during these six years of spiritual growth, and there are always new lessons from God.

Here is the bottom line for Julianne: It's all about letting God do His will in her life, as it is done in heaven. It is her pleasure to be a part of His work, and the showers of joy are not what she seeks. They are God's confirmation that what she sees taking place in front of her is coming from Him.

As your companionship with the Father grows richer and deeper, you will find that He is the one who makes things happen. He will transform you and you will transform the world. You will be directed by your heart. That is where everything must start. God works from the inside out. You will find that you can trust Him for guidance in everything that comes up, as He directs you to live from a transformed heart.

5

Healing for Wounded Hearts

IN THE NINTH CHAPTER of *Matthew* we find Jesus on a speaking tour, making guest appearances in all of the towns' and villages' synagogues. He was filled with tenderness because He saw that the crowds were "distressed and prostrate, like sheep without a shepherd" (*Matthew* 9:36). Throughout the region He had been healing those who were sick, and wherever He turned He found even more people in distress.

Welcome to the twenty-first century, Jesus. Things have not changed a bit. Suffering is everywhere, and we too are finding that folks are distressed and prostrate wherever we turn. Our best investigative efforts suggest that in the USA about a third of the women have been abused, and the rate among men is not much lower. In California, the numbers appear to be even higher—about half. The aftereffects of the widespread abuse are pervasive and, many times, devastating. School work fails, self-image drops, work history plummets, and there is not only a failure to thrive, but there is also a kind of chronic hopelessness.[1] It is as though the life of an abused person is a movie with the title, *You'll Never Make it, So Quit Trying.* Let's break that down into some practical numbers. If your church has 100 people at a gathering, at least 20 have been abused, and they have been struggling for their entire life from the aftereffects. In the USA there may be 60 million or more people whose lives have been seriously sidetracked by abuse. People are suffering everywhere we turn.

I know that you have spoken with these folks many times. They are acquaintances of yours, but they are usually very private about the abuse that they have been through. At times you may be able to sense that something is wrong, but you cannot bring yourself to talk about it with them.

---

1. U.S. Department of Health and Human Services Administration for Children and Families. *A Nation's Shame: Fatal Child Abuse and Neglect in the United States. A Report of the U.S. Advisory Board on Child Abuse and Neglect.* Fifth Report, April, 1995.

They cannot take their eyes off of the floor while talking, because they are filled with undeserved shame and guilt. They cannot trust that a friend will remain a friend, yet they deeply desire close friendships. Their hope is gone, and so is their confidence. They could use a shepherd.

If anything, the above description is an understatement, and it certainly does not exaggerate the picture. There are many, many people who want to get better, and they are determined to do so. Alcoholic's Anonymous meetings polka-dot your city. AA groups can be found in practically any city, morning, noon or night, every day. They are well attended, as are many unheralded meetings for other people who are in life-and-death battles with narcotics, obesity, anorexia, and relationship problems.

When it comes to religious abuse and spiritual abuse, the picture does not get any brighter. There is no accurate method available to get numbers concerning Satanic Ritual Abuse survivors, nor about Clergy Sexual Abuse survivors, but here is one telling indicator: Counselors' caseloads are full of folks with these devastating religious and spiritual nightmares.[2] Wounded hearts abound.

---

2. Although most of the information that we have about Satanic Ritual Abuse comes from victim reports, we have gained a lot of consistent information about it. An early study found that of 433 therapists, 134 were carrying out therapy for survivors of Satanic Ritual Abuse—and this study included only one city! (See *Ritual Abuse: Treatment, Intervention and Safety Guidelines.* Ritual Abuse Task Force, San Diego County Commission on Children & Youth, September, 1991.) That is about 30% of the therapists surveyed. Can you imagine the numbers if this rate were applied to the whole country? The problem is staggering. I was honored to join the Los Angeles Commission on Ritual Abuse, where I not only learned about the extent of this problem in my region, but spoke with therapists who are doing their best to help. (See *Ritual Abuse: Definitions, Glossary, The Use of Mind Control.* Report of the Ritual Abuse Task Force, Los Angeles County Commission for Women, 1994.) In the early 1990s, while preparing my first book, *Uncovering the Mystery of MPD,* I could find no suitable resource to document Satanic Ritual Abuse, so I included a chapter for that purpose. (See chapter 3: *Satanic Ritual Abuse.*) In my second book, *More Than Survivors: Conversations With Multiple-Personality Clients,* first released in 1992, I provided a chance for three SRA survivors to tell their stories—Crystal, Christina, and Keltie. The first-hand disclosures are hard to dismiss. Nonetheless, Satanic Ritual Abuse remains "hush-hush," it is covered up, denied, completely ignored by churches, and those of us who provide help for survivors get our fair share of criticism and threats. I have carried out treatment with about 50 SRA survivors, and have done diagnostic work with at least 50 others. It is clear that this area needs more helpers than are currently available.

We have also learned much about helping survivors of Clergy Sexual Abuse. Legal settlements with churches are running at about one million dollars per survivor, but those are mostly the teenage boy victims. What about the teenage girls, the younger children and the adult women? Where are the perpetrators? What about justice for them, and how about mercy for the survivors? There is a current awakening to this problem, and it looks

Jesus called out to His followers then, as He still does. "The harvest is plentiful, but there are few workers. So pray that the Lord of the harvest will thrust more workers into His harvest fields" (*Matthew* 9:37–38).

THE BATTLE FOR YOUR HEART

Cindi was convinced that there is something incurably wrong with her heart. A while back she told my answering machine that she needed to cancel her appointment, and may get in touch with me some day. When she finally did call me to set up another appointment, she could not promise that she "would be able to show up." She said that twice. Something in our last meeting had stirred up a long-standing spiritual dilemma. Nonetheless, she did show up at the new appointment. "If God gave me my heart," she blurted out as soon as she sat down, "isn't it all up to Him?" Despair and resignation had set in. There seemed no reason to keep on trying if God had given her a flawed heart.

A tormenting childhood experience had been uncovered during our previous meeting. Cindi had uncovered a memory of extreme abuse. What a flood of excruciating feelings that touched off. Talking logically with me about her heart helped her to manage those feelings. She explained to me that along with the tormenting memory, she had remembered a brief time of spiritual confusion in the middle of the memory that was practically impossible to understand. She had not told me about it while she was remembering it during the previous session because she could find no words to describe it at that time. She had hoped that the feelings about the memory would get better if she just ignored them, but they were becoming a little more upsetting each day. It was getting more difficult for her

as though we are going to find out that there are many more survivors of Clergy Sexual Abuse than any of us wants to believe. As is the case with Satanic Ritual Abuse, we find deep trenches dug around this issue, and there is extensive cover up. Often, when a pastor is identified as a perpetrator, he moves to a church in a different state, and the abuse charges remain confidential and legally hidden. He is free to live without his current congregation knowing his history of abuse, which leaves him free for further abuse. (See *The Sexual Abuse of Women by Members of the Clergy*, by Kathryn Flynn, 2003; *Is Nothing Sacred?*, by Marie fortune, 1989; and *How Little We Knew: Collusion and Confusion with Sexual Misconduct*, by Dee Ann Miller, 1993.)

If any people are distressed and prostrate, it is SRA and CSA survivors. They are desperate for support and have little reason to believe that they will gain assistance in their recovery. Most church help offered is no more than the proverbial drop in a bucket. For further first-hand information, you can visit websites on the internet from SRA and CSA survivors.

to ignore them. The *spiritual confusion* was bothering her even more than *remembering the torment*. She was definitely "going back and forth" about staying in therapy.

Here is what she told me about the spiritual confusion that had come up in the middle of the returning memory. While she was fearing death during the abuse, she saw a bright light that was very attractive. "It must be God coming to help me," she thought, and that brought her immense relief. However, she next sensed that she was pushed away from the light and believed that God was now rejecting her. She just had to ask me, "Why did He force me to remain in a body full of pain?" The battle for her heart was raging. She would rather be dead than to live in torment. The spiritual confusion was pulling her away from God, and she could only conclude that God was withholding His goodness from her. There was something about the torment that was keeping her from getting on with her life. She could only conclude that her heart must be damaged beyond repair.

Cindi has a remarkable gift for helping disabled children. There are certain kids in her school who respond only to her. Everybody on the team knows that, and they count on her to take care of the children that nobody else can reach. The kids sense that she is genuinely on their side, which helps them feel safe enough to open up to her.

"You told me, Jim, that I have a heart for children. But because of all that's going on inside of me, sometimes I cannot get out of bed and go to work. I just stay in my pajamas all day and I'm happy. I've been coming to you for over a year. I'm exhausted and I don't want any more pain. I'm telling God all the time that I want Him to fix my heart, but He doesn't make me feel any better."

We had come to the place where the mountain of pain was too high for her to climb alone, and she called out to God to prevent her from destroying herself. Suffering, motionless, waiting for an answer from God, she felt helpless, in a cloud of confusion.

I probably did not completely answer Cindi's question about her heart that day. Describing the pain in her heart was her way of saying how deeply she had been wounded. Talking logically with her about her heart was not enough to help her. She was desperate to get away from the pain that had been following her for her whole life. Would God, once again, draw her to Himself and then just reject her, as she had remembered? She sensed that because of what had happened during the abuse, that her heart is eternally lost.

It seemed to help Cindi a little when she began to realize that God had given her a heart for children. Following a brief time of prayer for healing the memory that contained the spiritual confusion, as we were talking about the kids she helps, she made a connection: God had taken her from being a wounded child to being a person who helps wounded children. The sparkle returned to her eyes. Her heart saw God in His mercy. After the prayer for healing, she was able to see that God has been helping wounded children through her. With the just-healed wound no longer clouding her vision, she began to see that God wants her to spread His goodness among wounded children. He has not given her a flawed heart. He has given her a heart for children, and it will guide her into carrying out His ministry among those kids.

THE HEART'S JOB

There are so many ways that people use the word "heart" in everyday conversations! Here are just a few that I have heard recently.

> "She does not have a mother's *heart.*"
> "You have a *heart* for ministry."
> "I love you with all my *heart.*"
> "My *heart* feels dead."
> "Let's get to the *heart* of the issue."
> "These are matters of the *heart.*"
> "That piano performance was technically good but it lacked *heart.*"
> "Since he quit his job as a pastor he has not been able to put his *heart* into his work."

The heart must be pretty important if it comes up so often at key points in conversations. Even when used in casual ways it implies a mysterious, unfathomable dimension. Many imponderable questions involve the heart. Questions like these:

> "Does love start in my *heart* or does love fill a mostly physical need?"
> "If romance fades, does that mean there's something wrong with my *heart*?
> "Can a *heart* be broken spiritually?"
> "Do feelings control my *heart*, or is it the other way around?"
> "Is the spiritual dimension of life only grasped by my *heart*?"
> "Does my *heart* come from God, or does it come from the choices that I make?"

Because of the unclarity in common usage it may seem a complete waste of time for you to consider the well being of *your heart* right now. I can understand your hesitancy. I once believed that the heart is a "gray area" topic myself. I saw no good reason to devote any time to a topic so subjective. For quite a while I decided to let other people talk about it—people who seemed to understand it better. I believed that I would be able to get along fine without taking the time to learn about my heart. It seemed too broad and elusive a topic to be fruitful.

Even though there are different ways in which people use the word, and even though those ways are not very precise, please keep this in mind: *The on-going battle for your heart* is something that you dare not ignore.

Your heart can be thought of as physical "eyes" that can see into the spiritual realm. It can help you *see what God has for you at any particular moment*. Here is a slice of life that illustrates how the heart works.

There are times that each of us can point to when we were seriously awe-struck with the wonders of the universe. From standing starry-eyed, overlooking the majestic Grand Canyon, to uncovering an intricate food chain teeming in your yard, to walking silently through a grove of redwoods, there are vivid snapshots that become imprinted in the minds of each of us.

When your *heart sees* such grandeur in God's creation there is a moment of tremendous appreciation, and your heart summons you to act accordingly. You are so taken with the magnificence of the created universe that you may rush out and buy a telescope before it gets dark, hoping to take a closer look at the flickering stars as soon as the sun sets. Or your heart could direct you to hurry over to your local nursery and buy a rose bush for your garden. You might be impelled to join a "save the whales" group, to organize your trip to the market around "recycling," or you may want to soak up a few verses from *The Psalms*. Maybe taking a walk in the park is what your heart directs you to do. "Come on, feed the ducks!" What you saw in the spiritual realm had a power-producing impact on your life, and your actions eagerly want to be directed by what you have seen spiritually. This can take place because your heart connects you to God's eternal world. The heart directs your actions. As we found in Jesus' teaching, living happens from the inside out.

What a very complicated question we have before us. "Was the idea about going to the park a thought, a feeling, a healthy habit or a message from God? Is there something He has for me at the park?" Just the *thought* that it is possible to have regular input from the spiritual realm in day-to-day life is a bit mind-boggling. Does the God who created it all care about what happens to me today, and will He direct me if I ask?

I, for one, have spent most of my life thinking about the spiritual realm as something that is pretty hard to integrate into my daily life. I have received religious teaching at regular times during the week, and have then gone about my life as though the lessons would somehow show up in my actions. I did not think very much about how the religious teaching could direct my moment-to-moment decisions. I knew the religious teachings well enough. Most of the time I thought of myself as a person who tries to follow biblical principles. That seems simple enough. To some extent, though, I was using my *head* to live, and not my *heart*. There was a lot of self-direction. There still is, but not as much.

My conscious desire was to be a loving person, and the Bible can certainly show me how to do that. The Bible teaches about love in many important passages. Beginners can get a lot from these passages, but it is also true that these teachings about love will always contain new nuggets of truth, no matter how many nuggets you may already have found. Some of the most inspiring sections of the Bible are about love, and there is always more that we can learn about love.

But then, to be fair, we *all* know that love is important, and we *all* know that we should try to be more loving, whether we read the Bible or not. Even *The Beatles* knew that. "All you need is love" is a memorable line from one of their big hits. Your mind will tell you that *The Beatles* were right. "Love is all you need." But the heart seeks to go much deeper. There is something eternally satisfying about love. We do not need to spend our lives singing simple phrases about love, hoping that "love" will help us feel good.

There is so much about love that God wants to give us. When we *try* to love in our own self-directed style, does it work? Not very well. God wants to maintain a connection with our hearts so that He can direct us into new arenas, where His love rules. As *The Sermon on the Mount* paints the picture, He wants to guide us into being people who display forgiveness, genuineness, peacefulness and sincerity from the inside out. This is where His love directs our life, and it can happen when our hearts are responsive to His guidance.

The heart's job is to make a connection with God, so that He can be active in every area of life—in every moment, in every activity and in every conflict. When your heart keeps you in sync with His direction, love happens from the inside out. Living in a heart aligned with Him allows Him to proceed with His work in and through you.

GIVING HIM CONTROL

There is no foolproof formula that tells people how to let God direct their every action. However, as *The Beatitudes* and *The Lord's Prayer* suggest, He is more than willing to get involved with those who invite Him. He is standing by, reaching out, ready to take their hand.

God reached out to Max in his early twenties. There was no church of any kind in his background, and he knew nothing about God, as presented in the Bible. His family was one of those underground cult families, whose lives were devoted to "a different god." The power of evil had cast a dark shadow over his family relationships. His ties to members of the cult group and to his extended family were fiercely loyal. One glaring weakness in cult ties is that they are inevitably based on fear. Cult loyalty is maintained by forcing children to attend rituals that promise future power. "You are chosen as our next exalted leader, so you must be trained." The training involves rituals with very high levels of fear. Here is the glaring weakness, their Achilles' heel: Since love is more attractive than fear, when God's love reaches cult-trained people, it is as refreshing as a summer shower. They have never before received love like that, and even a little bit will be more attractive than the cult leaders could ever imagine.

Max says he probably would have stuck with his family cult group, but a huge battle began inside of him when he accidentally stumbled onto a praise service that was taking place in his neighborhood. You may have heard the verse quoted, "Taste and see that the Lord is good" (*Psalm 24:8*). Well, that is exactly what happened to Max. Joyful, energetic music filled the air and beckoned to him. Singing praises to God, along with a room full of Christians, affected him in a way that he could not forget. He could taste God's presence. Eventually, he completely broke with his family's religion, and that was no small undertaking. It started with a small light in the darkness. God was there, and Max knew it. The sweet, sweet presence of Jesus beamed into his heart, and he began to look for ways to get God into every area of his life.

Some people sincerely seek the light, but in the wrong places. Tracy is a person who is very eager to share such a story. She grew up in a blended, multigenerational family, one where she did not receive enough hands-on affection. So her life developed under the cloud of neglect, which is always a deep wound. Worship was not a shared family tradition for her, as each member of her extended family had a different religion, including modern and ancient sects, with Mormonism and Catholicism added to the mix. For a brief time during her Jr. High School years her need to belong was wonderfully satisfied in the family of God. A Southern Baptist church gave her a taste of God's love, and she opened her heart to Him. But that church went through a ruthless split, marred by infidelity in the leadership, and she was left out in the cold. Tracy's heart had changed, but powerful factors pulled her away from the family of God. She started a new life in her 20's by moving to Southern California. The need to belong was begging to be met, and she began to seek God's love once again.

Tracy knew that there must be a gracious, good God out there somewhere. His loving touch could not be easily forgotten. However, Southern California has a hodgepodge of religious offerings, and Tracy began her search in the wrong places. Getting a lot of help from *new age* practitioners, and specifically from an organization devoted to combining all religions, her journey took some initial turns that seemed hopeful. Particularly promising was her venture to join a religion that originated in her ancestral homeland. She got in touch with some people from that group. It is not a hidden religion, just obscure, and she heard about this particular group after she had met some people from her home country. She was invited by these folks to join in "a little religious celebration." It was cozy and she began to sense that she could find some relief for her neglect wound in this setting. These were middle class people, comfortably dressed, celebrating a cultural anniversary. They were bringing in a little tradition, adding a little wine, and simply celebrating being closely knit people from that country. It was not very religious. It was a nice little get-together with cultural overtones, something friendly, and there was no fear on the scene.

After attending more gatherings over the next few weeks, Tracy was fitting in rather well. When it came time to celebrate the Summer Solstice, a big occasion for that group, plans were made to celebrate an afternoon ritual in a local park. They needed one more woman to take part in the traditional ceremony. She did not hesitate for a minute when they asked her ahead of time if she would join the leaders in a small circle, and take part, reading the traditional rites. June 21 came and about thirty people gathered around the seven leaders. They were dressed in traditional robes, standing in a circle. As she took her place among them, wearing a robe, Tracy began to sense that something terrible was about to happen. The leader hesitated and said that something was not right. His words were not exactly a warning, but they suggested that something unknown and fearful was rising up among them. Tracy did not know what the leader was talking about, even though the others seemed to know right away. The group got much quieter, and Tracy sensed that fear was definitely increasing among them.

She had been locked into a position she could not easily escape. Her fear was escalating and Tracy seriously wanted to back out. What would she tell the others who were ready to begin the ritual? She had been assigned to read a passage. She knew that she should back out, but there was also an urgency to please these people. After all, she had agreed to be one of the readers in the ritual. The internal battle ratcheted up a few notches. She began to shake, and could barely read her lines. Anxious, almost to the point of terror, the next few minutes slipped by in a blur, as though she was in some kind of a spell. Her feelings had been tampered with, and there was no getting away from the terror that was being stirred up in her.

She did not recover when she reached her home that evening. Disjointed and anxious, Tracy was unable to negotiate her world. She could not go to work, and a few days later, after her doctor's meds did not help, she was miraculously led to an internist. That doctor knew how to treat the rare disease that she had contracted. She would have been dead in a few days without that particular doctor's specialized understanding. But even the right medical intervention did not end her terror. Recovering, but still terrorized, she attended a local church. It turned out to be in a language that was foreign to her. She did not have any idea what was being sung or spoken during that evening service. However, she clearly knew that she was being led to stay there until the end of the meeting. Then a woman who spoke fairly good English began to talk to her, and turned as white as a sheet. She called to a few of her friends nearby and they began to pray for Tracy. They prayed about witchcraft and demons that evening. They also went to her house the next day and prayed against "the paganism" lodged there. From that point forward, Tracy's heart was changed.

When I asked Tracy what she wants me to include if I ever share her story, she said two words—"dangerous" and "deceitful." "Dangerous" is easy to explain. She literally teetered on the brink of death, and her emotional life was destroyed until she renounced her ties to that false religion. Tracy told me that I cannot emphasize this point too much. Your eternal well being and your life itself are at serious risk if you dabble in false religions. A person doesn't have to dive into a cesspool to discover what's in it.

It is not as easy to describe how "deceitful" that group was, and how insidious the aftereffects were. When the group opened their arms to her, Tracy had no way of preparing herself for the spiritual takeover that awaited her. By the time she realized that she needed to escape, she was already in the snare.

Tracy was looking for a God who would bless her, and would meet her deep need to belong that had been unmet since the Southern Baptist church fell apart. When she sought God in the wrong places, terror and death visited her. That is the way Satan is—he stalks like a lion, preying upon people who are wounded, and Tracy had a deeply hurting neglect wound. I met Tracy shortly after she joined our church choir, only a half year after her heart was changed in the foreign language church. While she was telling me all about the Summer Solstice event, she was speaking about it with a sense of completion. It seemed to be over, and she was eager to tell people to watch out—"don't ever stray from the straight and narrow path."

A few weeks later I got a call from her, and she needed to talk with me right away. She hurried over to my office. She could not focus at work because the terror that began at the ritual was building up inside of her again. I asked her to recall whatever she could remember about the ritual, to "climb into the moment" when she was in the ritual circle, and to try to remember what it was like during that trance state. As she opened up to what had happened she began to shake again, some of the terror returned, and she remembered being wrenchingly taken over by a spirit. After re-living the ritual event, she renounced the spirit, and we asked God to bring an end to the terror. The sweet, sweet presence of Jesus filled the room. Her heart had urged her to meet with me, and we uncovered the wound that contained the terror. God's light dispelled the darkness that had remained as an aftereffect from the ritual. Her heart was doing its job, letting God provide direction. Now, a year later, the shaking and the terror have not returned. Her need to belong is again being met in the family of God. God was with her at the brink of death, and is now with her in the flow of her life. She has given control of her life to a gracious, good God who has delivered her from evil.

DELIVERANCE FROM EVIL

The first chapter of *I Peter* has a lot of very important information to digest, and it takes a bit of devoted study to get to the bottom of that passage. When I first looked at it I did not realize that it was addressed to people who needed deliverance from evil. I was stumped when I came to the word "sojourners," which is used twice in that chapter, so I gave my brother a phone call.

I am a very fortunate person. My brother is a biblical language specialist. He is a professor at a major University, so he keeps his Greek and Hebrew language skills sharp. That helps me a lot because I can ask him questions whenever I get stumped about a scripture passage.

His explanation about being a sojourner helped me to understand, to some extent, the life-and-death struggle of the early Christians to whom Peter's letter was written. My brother started by telling me that some translations completely miss the point that Peter is making when he used that word. They substitute words like *aliens* or *strangers* for the Greek word, *sojourners*, apparently trying to use words that the reader will be more familiar with. It is crucial to point out that Peter specifically addressed this letter to sojourners (verse 1). Understanding that word will be a big help in explaining the first chapter, and the rest of the letter as well. *I Peter* was written to *sojourners*.

The question that I asked my brother came up because of verse 17. "What is Peter saying about living life as a sojourner in reverent awe?" My brother told me that in the Roman Empire each city was governed by its *citizens*. They were an elite class of people, usually less than ten percent of the population. The citizen families had lived on their estates for generations, had businesses, owned slaves and were automatically granted reverence by those who were not a citizen. It is essential to keep in mind that only citizens had legal rights. They were the only people protected under the law. There were instances, as was the case for the Apostle Paul, where a person could become a citizen for reasons other than family lineage, but those were the exceptions, not the rule.

Sojourners had no rights. They were the working class. By far, the majority of the people who lived in that society were sojourners. They had no legal protection from citizens, who could be unpredictable and dangerous at the drop of a hat. Sojourners usually scraped by with no guarantee that they could obtain even the bare essentials from day to day. "Please help me not to worry about my daily bread" was their earnest prayer. They had no family doctor, had no health insurance, no retirement account, and there was no one to defend them if they got into trouble. It takes quite a leap for my Western mind to wrap around that idea—no rights.

Sojourners were blue-collar workers, had respectable jobs, and some were even skilled artisans. They were the backbone of the culture. And yet to the citizens, they were considered almost sub-human. They were looked down upon, and often despised. Definitely in a lower class than the citizens, sojourners' lives were not valued, so they were never safe. To violate the religious customs in their city could bring a death sentence. The citizens' estates were dedicated to the city's gods, and were set up with shrines and altars at the entry points to their houses. Every time they passed through those gates, sojourners were required to present a sacrifice to their highly revered gods. To refuse this demand could cost a sojourner his life, or there could be other cruel punishments. Sojourners had to be kept in line. They could be summarily executed, which would be an ominous warning to other sojourners who may have ideas about dishonoring the city's gods.

Now we are starting to see what Peter's letter is all about. To be a follower of Christ could cost a sojourner his life. "You worship a Hebrew god? You refuse to make a sacrifice to my god when you enter my estate? That is not okay. Off with your head." No wonder Peter's call was for sojourners to live their lives in reverent awe. Their lives were so easily discarded. It is hard for me to imagine living each day with that kind of a threat hanging over my head. In my Western mind, practicing a religion cannot be forced on a person, as was the case in the Roman Empire. A sojourner should at least sincerely believe in the city's religion before being required to participate in it. How ridiculous it is for me to think that a person would be risking his life by withholding a sacrifice to the local god. There was no justice, no back-up plan, no higher power, and there was no certainty that a Christian sojourner would see tomorrow.

While we were discussing this passage in a home Bible study meeting, trying to understand what life is like for a sojourner, Nathaniel told us his story. He was raised in a Christian village in a Muslim nation. His account may not be politically correct but it needs to be told. He is a sojourner.

Nathaniel told us it is wonderful that Christians are allowed to meet openly in this country. He could hardly believe that there are so many home Bible study groups. It is, however, strikingly hard for Nathaniel to understand that we give Muslim people the right to freely practice their religion. He cannot believe that the two groups of people can live together in peace. In his country, hundreds of Christian ministers were murdered when radical Muslims took over the government. Thousands of churches were burned and some Christian villages were completely exterminated and wiped off of the map. Nathaniel said that some of the radical Muslims in his country would like to kill every person, worldwide, who is non-Muslim—called "infidels"—and replace the present governments all over the world with their radical leaders. Nathaniel could not fathom that we are protecting their right to meet in private, considering the motives that could lead them to violence. He assured us that it is only a matter of time, and we will see the truth about the danger that we are in. Terror has not yet begun, as he sees it, but it will certainly begin at some point. He has had more than enough personal experience with extremists in his country, and he can imagine what they could do.

Having grown up in a Christian village, all of Nathaniel's family and friends were in danger when the radical Muslim government was established. As was the case in other countries that have been strictly ruled by Muslim extremists, there are no rights. There is no democracy, no way to appeal for justice when Christians are executed, there is no free press, and the ruling class can kill practically anyone they want. Nathaniel was a modern day sojourner, as soon as the extremists took over in his country.

At that time Nathaniel was studying at a university in the nation's capital. He had heard about the mass executions of pastors and Christian villagers that were taking place in other parts of the country, so he organized a protest group in his university to try to attract some international attention from the press about the on-going atrocities. He was immediately rounded up, along with the other protesters, and jailed. *I Peter* was written to Nathaniel. His life was in danger. Repeatedly tortured and completely convinced that he would soon be killed, he was unexpectedly freed after only a few days. His story is a bit like the Apostle Peter's, who was unexpectedly released from prison and showed up at the house where people were praying for him to get out of jail.

And what did Nathaniel do as soon as he was released? He went back to organize another protest. That is not what I would do. But an international peace organization snapped him up for his protection just before the next protest, and flew him out of the country. How he ended up here is a series of practically impossible circumstances. So far, you only have a brief outline of the events that shaped his heart. While being tortured he was certain he was about to be killed. Those moments would be enough to shake any person to the core. "Why did I survive? How did God get me out of there?"

His story continued and we listened in rapt attention. Shortly after his escape from his home country, when Nathaniel was hoping to get a United States visa at a European consulate, his deeply held faith had become his lifeline. Having heard of the one-in-a-thousand odds that he would be permitted to get such a visa, he prayed earnestly, all night long. At that point there was only one option, should he be denied a USA visa—he would be flown back to his country, where he would be summarily executed. Actually *getting* that particular kind of a visa was unheard of. It was also unheard of for a person to be cleared for entry into the USA from the European city he had landed in.

On the morning after spending a night in prayer, he walked right into the consulate, and no questions were asked. He was immediately approved and came straight to our country. Even though he had no contacts here, he was on his way. It was a gripping story, to be sure. I will not forget his soft-spoken voice that told us about all of these God-ordained openings in his life. Never for a second drawing attention to himself, he simply spoke *in reverent awe* of a God who is really in charge of this world. It was right then that I learned the answer to my question about the meaning of *I Peter* 1:17. "Live your lives as sojourners in reverent awe." When our very lives are on the line His power directs circumstances, and we find Him at work all around us—in our living space.

And I will also long remember the Bible study meeting that took place a few weeks prior to that. It was before I had heard about God's miraculous hand in getting Nathaniel to our country. The people in the Bible study group had been praying that he would get a job that had just opened up in a big firm. He had been working for minimum wages ever since entering our country. Being a highly intelligent person with university training, he should be able to get a white-collar job, with good pay and benefits. We all believed that this job opening would be perfect for him. If we prayed, we could trust that God would come through. At the next meeting we asked Nathaniel whether he had been offered the job. He smiled broadly, and said how thankful he was for our prayers. Still smiling, he told us that he did *not* get the job, without departing from his soft-spoken demeanor. That is the part I will long remember. When I am desperate I tell God what to do for me. Nathaniel apparently had given God control of his life, and was able to trust that God is in control, even when he was asking God for something that was pretty urgent.

When Nathaniel told us he had prayed through the night, just before going in for the interview, at first I wondered if that could be true. Who would get that serious about prayer? I thought that perhaps it was his way of saying he had a long prayer time and went to bed pretty late. I would run out of words long before the morning light. Wouldn't you? Not departing from his steady, soft-spoken tone, he went on. "I am very pleased that God did not give me that job," he said. "God must have something better for me."

Nathaniel's words stand as a challenge to those of us who believe that we know God's intentions for our life. "God must have something better for me." Later, after I found out how God had intervened to spare his life by helping him escape from his home country, I began to sense how Nathaniel's heart had been transformed. God had delivered him from evil. He had faced death. He had suffered and survived. His heart became like a child's heart. It was full of faith, the faith that God is truly in control all of the time. He was delighted that God had answered all of our prayers with a firm, "No." His heart was doing its job. He was firmly convinced that God always guides his steps, and was fully satisfied that God's direction will always be good.

I tend to tell God what He should do for me. "Call on Him and He will grant your request," is a very popular notion. That kind of prayer can be more like bargaining with God than seeking His will. "Wouldn't you like for me to have a nice house in a quiet neighborhood, God? If you give me one, I will be a better light in your world, so please, Lord, how about putting me in a better house? Even a little bit bigger would be fine, Lord. I don't like where you have put me."

That is not really a "Christian" approach to prayer. That is not faith at all. That is "looking out for number one." I know that I am supposed to make my prayer a *request*. I should make the request *in Jesus' name* and leave the rest up to Him. But when my heart is not attuned to God, I am actually asking Him to grant my requests on the basis of *my own interests*. In the Middle Eastern world of Jesus' time, perhaps they understood this a little better, but even the people that Jesus met probably struggled with the same question that I struggle with. *Can I really give God control of my life to the point where what He wants is exactly what I want? The Lord's*

Prayer gives us His direction for our prayers: "Please take control in every area of my life and guide me here on earth, just as You are in control of everything in heaven."

Here is an analogy that I picked up from a Sunday school teacher about twenty years ago. It is one of those ideas that still pops into my mind every once in a while. It is a challenging perspective that I cannot quit thinking about. The Sunday school teacher was trying to apply a scripture, and I regret that I do not remember what passage he was explaining. He said that we should think about the place we live in military terms. Wherever our home is, is exactly where we have been posted in God's war. God is the Five Star General and we are all Privates. Do we tell Him where we are supposed to be posted? Do we send Him orders about which military base He should transfer us to? The General knows the battle plan, and he has positioned us right where he wants us. Now, about twenty years later, Nathaniel's story has helped me to see the point that the Sunday school teacher was trying to make. When my heart is lined up with God it will not occur to me to tell God that He has made a mistake, and it will be easier to thank Him for whatever happens. Even if I am devastated because of unexpected developments, I may be able to accept that "God must have something better for me."

Here is what you want to be able to say to yourself. "Whatever He wants is what I want. If I invite Him, He will work with me to give me what is best, even when I do not see it right away."

His work in a person's life begins in the heart, and from there it makes its way into every aspect of life. Talking everything over with the Father gives Him permission to take control, and to deliver us from evil. That is how Cindi, Max, Tracy and Nathaniel have discovered that He works.

WOUNDS AND HEARTS

Here is what we have learned about the heart so far. It wants to direct our actions. If your actions are not God-honoring, your heart is probably not healthy enough to do its job. Even if your heart starts to push you in the right direction, if it is weaker than the other forces in your life, it is not healthy enough to do its job—connecting you to God. At these "battle for your heart" moments, your heart cannot direct your actions because it is too wounded. The heart *informs* your actions but cannot *direct* them.

An example from a mature, godly man seems to fit. Joe had found a classic cowboy movie in a video store, and was definitely going to watch it when he got home. His heart? It wasn't part of the picture yet. He sat down and watched the cowboy movie right away, even though signals from his wife were not favorable. She needed to talk to him when he got home, but he could not think about anything other than watching the movie that he had just rented.

After a fight between them ended on a very sour note, he pulled sullenly away. Now it was a few days later, and things were still not good at home. When I asked Joe about his heart, he immediately realized what had happened. He said it was a spiritual problem, in that he was not turning to God about watching the movie. He lost his balance, as contempt emerged rather abruptly, and that is what started the fight. His search for God's guidance was being blocked when he most needed it.

"Just where do you find that contempt coming from?" I asked.

We found a wound that started with repeated beatings from an older brother, and it needed some healing before he was able to regain his balance. The contempt for his brother was being directed toward his wife, and blocked his heart's influence altogether. After that wound received some prayer and healing, his heart informed him to go straight home to correct his error. Was that a problem between him and his wife? It seems to have been a heart problem that turned into a relationship problem because of an unhealed wound. It was not a problem that he was conscious of, at least until we uncovered being beaten by his brother, but it was a powerful force, nonetheless. He had lost the battle for his heart when contempt directed him more powerfully than his heart. He was living in his hurt because of unresolved contempt.

Here is the way it looks to me. An unhealed wound can seriously interrupt daily life. Even a healthy heart can have its work blocked by unresolved feelings, as was the case for Joe. It takes healing of the wounds and it takes a heart aligned with God. When your heart does its job, getting you *connected* to God, what does He show you about the forces that compete with your heart to control your life? Are there wounds back there somewhere that can, at times, be more powerful than your heart? Do they produce hopelessness, contempt, lust, dishonesty, retaliation or false righteousness? As those wounds receive His healing, the Father will strengthen your heart. When more of your wounds are healed, your heart will be more able to receive His guidance, unhindered.

There is a movie that has been playing in your head since your earliest days. It has some scenes in it that block His guidance. They are scenes with conflicts and wounds. They will need to be edited.

6

The Movie in Your Head

W HAT MAKES PEOPLE TICK? What is it that causes them to get into a certain routine and live their life in a particular way? Why do they sense that they are duty-bound to eat a certain kind of food, or to exercise so many minutes each day, or to have devotions at a particular time, or to faithfully visit family members who despise them? Especially when it seems that they are stuck on a merry-go-round, with upsetting feelings regularly re-surfacing, just why is it so hard to jump off, and live differently?

There is a movie that keeps playing in your head that tells you how to live. It shows you scenes from your past, it creates dreams about your future, and it nudges you to follow the script. We have been trained about how to live, beginning in our earliest days, and we will continue to be stuck in a particular script unless there is a conscious effort to change it. Some of the movie's traumatic scenes pack a powerful punch, and prevent the movie from going in a new direction. The movie's title can be daunting, something like, "The Loser," "The Invisible Person," "Just Shoot Me!" or "Men are Monsters." People whose script resists change can sense that they are on a merry-go-round, and the traumatic episodes keep being relived, over and over, in their on-going life.

"I give up. You know that I've been trying to find a new family. When I find new Christian friends I get a little hopeful. It's okay for a while, but then everyone leaves without saying a single word. As a child I was always lonely and that hasn't changed a bit."

Discouragingly, the new scenes being lived out are just as hard to tolerate as the originals. That is exactly what happens on the merry-go-round. Past and present seem exactly the same. The most painful wounds are near the surface, and they are easily re-injured in new situations. The re-injured wounds produce exactly the same feelings, and that makes it seem so clear that "I will always feel this bad. Here is another hopeless scene, just like every other scene." The movie script firmly resists being changed. The merry-go-round completes another cycle.

We keep hearing that people have choices, but it does not really seem that is so. Recurring dreams about absent family members, nightmares that produce enough gloom to spoil a day, anxiety that will not stop, headaches of all kinds, bodily aches and pains, feelings that make it impossible to get out of bed, and being held in the grip of a no-win situation—these have nothing to do with choices. They come directly from shadowy scenes in a person's movie, in the scenes that keep replaying. The unwanted pain from unhealed wounds steadily intrudes into daily life, and people have no idea where to find relief.

So what makes people tick? They would like to be in a much better movie. Even if they do not think of it in this way, they want to overcome the effects of the traumatic scenes and they want to create new, joy-filled scenes. The upsetting scenes keep getting played inside because they hope to turn out better each time. That is what makes people tick. They are looking for a new start. They want to live a far better life.

The main point that Jesus developed in the first half of *The Sermon on the Mount* helps people to believe that they can create a new movie. We see there that wounded heart problems can keep a person living in scenes, where the same wound brings out the same suffering day after day. The traumatic experiences that produce hopelessness, contempt, lust, dishonesty, retaliation and false righteousness will do their best to stop the new scenes from turning out better. Here is what Jesus' sermon suggests: Talk it all over with the Father.

> Please take control in every aspect of my life, just as you are in control of heaven. Please heal my heart's wounds. Transform it so that I can become a person who bears your family resemblance. Guide me so that I will automatically be forgiving, genuine, peaceful and sincere, and will become a person whose heart shows love to everyone.

MANAGEMENT AND HEALING

Overcoming the effects of the heart's wounds is a central idea in living a far better life. *People can either manage their wounds or they can seek healing for them.* There are not many other choices. Developing routines and living a predictable life are common ways to help keep upsetting feelings manageable. In high stress situations, calling on a friend, seeking comfort, or enjoying spiritual recovery are all methods to manage feelings, and that is an absolute necessity. Anxiety, hopelessness and jealousy, for example, are overwhelming even in a very short span of time, and people need to *do something*. Painful feelings will surely show up on your landscape, like craters on the moon, and you will have to deal with them. Management is good, but if the intruding feelings can be healed, that is even better.

Try to think of "management and healing" as though you have a thorn in your foot. You can limp, and leave the thorn in, if it is properly bandaged, or you can pull it out. There may be quite a bit of pain when you extract a deeply embedded thorn, but it leaves no lasting pain or infection after it has been taken out. I see too many people limping, saying they are just fine, but their actions show that they are not okay. It would be a good idea for them to get the thorn out.

There is a pandemic of addictions in our culture these days, and it may be good to use "addictive conditions" to illustrate the difference between management and healing. The first point to consider is that people with an addiction have something painful that they must deal with in one way or another. If they use prescription pain killers or sleep aids, these may help in the short run, but may lead to an addiction. The same can be said for eating, smoking, alcohol or drug addiction, and it may also be said for computer addiction, sexual addiction and pornography addiction. These all change the blood chemistry in a "feeling better" way. As stated, there is an immediate benefit, but there is a downside in the long run. Addiction is a management tool, in that it helps to manage something, like anxiety, depression, bodily pain and a wide variety of life-long defensive patterns, and an addiction may make it unnecessary to seek healing.

Please do not take the idea lightly, about how to understand addictive disorders. They are pain management strategies. We all need to get past 12-step approaches and the cognitive-behavioral approaches, and get some documented, scientific insight about what is really going on with addictions. I was fortunate to attend a seminar in February of 2007.[1] This was presented by the highly esteemed professor, Dr. Allan Schore. His incredible breadth of knowledge in the science and the art of psychotherapy left about 300 of us clinicians practically breathless, during his two-day presentation. His astute points, one after another, kind of flew by in front

1. Allan N. Schore. *The Science of the Art of Psychotherapy*. UCLA David Geffen School of Medicine, February, 2007.

of us without any fanfare. We all knew that we were getting the most current material available, material that can give us approaches that have the best chance of helping people. He covered quite a range of material, using 344 power point slides—what a boatload of information that was.

In the middle of that wealth of information, near the end of the first day, he covered "the effects of pathological dissociation, a primitive defense against overwhelming affects." He said that pathological dissociation, cutting everything off because it is overwhelming, is a key feature in a list of widespread conditions. On the list were "eating disorders" and "substance abuse and alcoholism." It is now clear that scientists and counselors are saying the same thing. There is no longer any doubt. Addictions come from a thorn, and there is a history of using pathological dissociation to deal with the thorn. Here is the bottom line for addicts: When they "get better" it is because they have gotten the thorn out, not because they have learned how to live with it. Management of addictive conditions will result in periodic relapse, until the thorn is removed. I want to see people healed, not urged to stay in a management lifestyle, where they need to keep on using pathological dissociation. After healing, if the problem-producing trigger pops up again there will no longer be any need to turn to the addiction. That is living a better life.

If you cannot manage, you need healing. Try to manage your day by keeping some helpful Bible verses in your mind, talk about them with key people and talk about them with God. Put your best, God-directed effort into managing your life. If, under those conditions you cannot keep going in your intended direction, it is probably because you have a pocket of pain somewhere, hidden by pathological dissociation, that is too intense to be managed. Pain that resists management and interrupts your day needs to be healed. If the unhealed wound continues to produce unmanageable feelings, it will pull you in the wrong direction until you find healing.

Here is a classic case of how management was not working for one person. A Sunday School teacher—a very sincere, godly man—was in an unmanageable, merry-go-round pattern. Jerold said that he had prayed about what to work on with me at this session, while he was driving to my office. I asked if he had any recent problems where his feelings were interfering in his daily life. Following further prayer, he remembered how he was feeling last Sunday morning, his eyes narrowed and he instantly began to feel the unmanageable fear again. He said that on some Sundays, before class begins, he gets all tied up in exactly this same fear before walking into the Sunday School room.

"I imagine that the room is practically empty, or that the usual people will be missing. But then I give it to God." He went on to describe how that even though he has given it to God many times, when he enters the Sunday School room, he is often still "tied up in fear."

"What is '*it*,'" I asked?

At first he did not understand my question. I was trying to get him in touch with the feeling that blocked him just before he entered the Sunday School room. After I had explained this more fully to him, he connected to the feelings he was struggling with just before Sunday School. "*It*" is the fear about nobody showing up, he told me. This led him to experience the unmanageable feeling again. He put the fear into words. "Loss. Empty. That's it." He began to feel very small, tears swelled up in his eyes, and he could sense that he was remembering crying in his crib. I encouraged him to stay in touch with the crib experience.

"What happened? What are you seeing and hearing?"

All that he could sense at first was a prolonged sadness and aloneness. Then he said, "I don't know if this is true, but my dad comes in and he's mad." Moment by painful moment the episode continued. At each new second of the story, whatever happened next was a surprise to Jerold. He was trying to stop crying, just like his father was asking him to, but he could not stop. The father soon picked him up and began shaking him, not very hard at first, but harder and harder, as the crying continued. He then tossed little Jerold back into the crib. He was crying, out of control, and he received no desperately needed comfort. As he continued to let the early memory emerge, his feelings built up and were eventually released. As the memory of the incident came to its end, Jerold got in touch with the emptiness that followed the shaking.

Here is the story. At first he was a baby crying in his crib, then he was shaken by an out-of-control dad, and finally he was left alone, without comfort. We discovered exactly what had been interfering with Sundays— it was the uncomforted emptiness at the end of the abuse episode. There was a small pocket of pain back there that kept coming up because it wanted to be healed. When it "came up," Jerold felt the despairing emptiness. We prayed that God would heal the wounds from that incident, and give lasting comfort.

Jerold had no previous conscious memory of this "baby shaking incident," but that did not stop us from praying that God's healing would come to him in that hidden pocket of pain. We had prayed for God to give him something to talk about at this session's start. We began by looking at a fear that interferes with his calling as a Sunday School teacher, found the origin of the fear, and ended by offering prayer for healing the wound. Did it help? Jerold's life no longer is bothered by the childlike fear on Sundays. As Jesus said, "You will know a tree by its fruit." If we prayed about it and it had a good effect, it appears that healing took place. Jerold no longer had to "give it to God" before entering the Sunday School room. "*It*" had received healing and there was no longer was any fear, waiting to be managed. Hopelessness had been pulling at his heart, but now was healed. We extracted the thorn, and he is no longer limping.

"So is the problem supposed to be gone now," he asked? Jerold deeply wanted that to be the case.

"We will see," I replied. That is my usual answer to that frequently asked question. "If the problem comes back, there is probably some other aspect of the wound that is not yet healed. We will be able to seek healing for that as well. For now, let's just thank God for His help with today's problem."

The movie in Jerold's head no longer has a "baby shaking incident" in it, that brought along the fear and hopelessness, that can sidetrack him on Sundays. In fact, each scene that Jerold re-works becomes a scene in his new movie, one that God is editing. Creating a new movie to replace the old one is what it takes to live a far better life.

THE JESUS CHANNEL

Re-working old scenes and creating new ones can take place in a dramatic fashion or it can stay fairly casual. This process can help with deeply embedded problems, where there can be very strong feelings, or re-working the scenes may seem like nothing more than teaching a lesson.

Let me tell you about a little episode where my five-year-old granddaughter worked through some feelings and learned how to change her inner movie. When she was visiting us recently, she came down the stairs crying, shortly after she had gone to bed. I picked her up, about half of the way down, and asked her what was wrong.

Still sobbing, she explained. "I can't stop the Marios, Grampa, and the sounds won't go away, and I'm gonna' have bad dreams all night!" (There is a video game where little "Marios" relentlessly consume everything that is in their way.)

After I had gotten her back into bed, and we had prayed a few "thank you prayers," I told her that I wanted her to try to see something. "Jesus told people to not stop the children from coming to Him. He knew that they wanted to, and when they came to Him, He welcomed them with His arms wide-open, blessed them and let them sit on His lap. Then He told everyone that they should never hurt the kids."

"Really, Grampa? He said that?"

"He sure did. It's in the Bible in three different places. He probably said that a lot of times to a lot of people. Can you see Him doing that?"

"Yes, Grampa."

"Good. That's good. Now, in case those Mario pictures come back, here is what you can do. There is a Mario channel, but you can switch over to the Jesus channel. You know, you can watch the Jesus channel any time you want."

That was the end of her troubles for the evening. She slept fine, and none of us thought to ask her how she was doing the next morning, because she was her sparkly little self as soon as she got out of bed.

Later in the day, as she was about to get into the car and go back home, she called out to me. "Grampa! I can watch the Jesus channel any time I want." She got it. There is an eternal truth that people can grasp at any age. God is always sending His personalized airwaves down to us, and whenever we need to we can switch over to His channel. That is, pretty much, the same thing that Jesus said about the Father being right next to us in the Kingdom of the Heavens. Whenever you need Him you can watch His channel or invite Him to join you in your living space. However you want to think about it, He is there for you *whenever*.

Giving people the idea that they can switch over to the Jesus channel seems to put a new spark in their eyes. It has immediate appeal, and it is supported by scripture. Here are two references. In 2 Corinthians 10:4-7, Paul says that the weapons we fight with are more powerful than human weapons. They have God's power to overthrow lies and logic, and whatever defies the knowledge of God. We can take every thought captive, and make it obedient to Christ. I would say that is very much like asking

God to help us turn on the Jesus channel, where the truth is proclaimed all of the time.

The other reference is one of my favorites. It is found in 2 Corinthians, chapter 3. Paul refers to an Old Testament story, when Moses spent some time with God on a mountaintop, just before he came down with the Ten Commandments. Paul points out that Moses' face was glowing so brightly, following his time with God, that folks could not even look directly at him. So Paul says to his readers that since Jesus has come, we all have access to God, in the same way that Moses did, and we can expect to glow too. In fact, God continues to transform us, and we get a little brighter as we stay close to Him. I believe that Paul would agree that the more time we spend with God, the more we let Him stay close to us and direct our lives, the more light we will give off. When we glow, that's good. When we spend time looking at the Jesus channel, that's good. It tells us how to live. Watching the Jesus channel can be a method of providing both management and healing, because it keeps a person going in the right direction and brings God's healing into the picture. Your inner movie may need a little re-writing, and introducing a few scenes from the Jesus Channel may help a lot.

REWRITING YOUR SCRIPT

Let me go over a conversation that I had on the phone this morning. It is a good illustration of the way that inner movies can get changed. Dorrie had been on the urgent help line, trying to find someone who would prevent her from hurting herself. That was an understatement. She was going back-and-forth about killing herself. God be praised, she found the right person, to get her through the immediate crisis. Now, two days later, she was ready to try to get some healing for the wound that urged her to kill herself. My hope was to get her in touch with the painful feelings.

"So do you have an idea what got you into the self-destruct mode two days ago?"

"No. I don't even remember."

We prayed that God would give us enough light to find out what the problem is.

"Is it okay if we go back to something I have already talked about?" she asked.

"Sure," I replied. "If something is painful there, that means there is more that needs to be healed. Please tell me what you were seeing and hearing back there. Was there a different time in your life when you felt this way?"

"There were a lot of times. My father hurt me, my husband hurt me and God hurt me, when I was small, and for all of my life."

"Try to get back as far as you can. Whatever you can remember about that kind of hurt early in your life, is what you want to zoom in on. Tell me what you see."

"I see a baby in the hospital."

"What do you know about her?"

"She is afraid of her father and mother. The parents are fighting. It's real loud."

Dorrie speaks out what she is hearing. "'You made me have this brat.' 'Just keep your legs together, (the B word).' She replies. 'I'm not going to take care of her, so it's up to you.' The mom continues. 'I can't stand her!'"

Dorrie says the scene changes. "And I'm seeing mom in the shower. She's screaming at me. I'm in her tummy, and she's hitting me and hitting me until she's black and blue."

"That has to be as hard as anything, when your mother wants to get rid of you."

"Ya' think?"

"What else can you see there?"

"When the staff people pick her up she is really happy."

"So a part of her is joyful and another part of her is fearful—the part who knows the parents?"

"Yah. She is so afraid of them."

After a considerable time of silence, I continued. "We've found some scenes during earlier sessions, where her father violated her whenever he wanted to, and the mother did nothing to protect her. It seems to have started out when she was really young."

Dorrie continued to be quiet.

"You have been watching an inner movie with some scenes in your life from when you were very small. It was a terrible time—a violent dad, an absent mom, and the part of you that has some joy was nowhere around. Let's ask God to get some healing to the wounds that just now opened up. 'Dear Lord, what an awesome God you are. Thanks for helping us find these two wounded young ones, the fearful one and the joyful one.

84

Please restore them. We ask you to wash them with your living water, heal their wounds, provide divine comfort and deliver them from evil. Please bring that chapter of Dorrie's life to a close, and open up a new chapter for her, where you can bring people into her life who care for her. Please restore the joy for the part who knew what joy was like way back then, and bring an end of suffering for the one who was despised.'"

After a pause, I asked if she could please let me know how she's doing.

"A lot better, but I've got some questions about God. He's a little late to protect me, isn't He?"

I could see that Dorrie had been delivered from the evil in that pocket of pain, and she immediately had begun to work on the questions that surround the event. Why did God let it happen in the first place?

"Those people were going to hurt you no matter what God did," I said. "His hope is to restore you now, so the pain can finally stop. And He's bringing new people into your life to bless you." (I mentioned three supportive people that she had previously told me about.)

Just a few seconds later, she responded. "That's right. There is a new movie."

Using the idea that life can be like a movie that can be edited, seems to give people a little hope, and a little direction in their efforts to live a better life. Here is an example that shows what this looks like. One person was not ready to talk about "changing her script" until she was well down the road to re-working her wounds. Trish did not want to see anyone for therapy—period. Her friends had to practically hog-tie her and bring her in! But now, after a few key wounds have been healed, she has no problem with the whole idea of continuing to seek healing for her wounds whenever they interfere.

Before we first got together, she quizzed me about my approach, and we came to agree that we would pray for the healing of painful memories. We would avoid talking endlessly about her mom, as a previous therapist had done. She had enough conscious memories to work on, and we found other wounds to pray about each time she came in. Having missed a few weeks of talking with me, she came into one session in an awful dither. "Nobody helps. They just stand around and do nothing."

After prayer for God's guidance, we were led to a memory that she did not know about in her conscious mind. That was a pocket of pain that was well hidden by pathological dissociation. It opened up, as a movie scene does, complete with sky-high anxiety, serious bodily pain and a time of no comfort after the end of abusive incident. It was being raped by a stranger in a junior high school room, followed by a scene with people crowding around her who did not give her any help. She was confused, speechless, and wanted to get away as soon as possible. That was a huge pocket of pain, and it was bleeding into her present day life. There was the anxiety, the body pain and the certainty that nobody would help her. Re-working the memory and asking for God to supply His divine comfort to close up the wound had remarkable effects. Now that the wound no longer sends anxiety to her, and now that there is no longer the isolating sense that nobody will help, Trish is doing quite well.

In assessing what made the difference, she said that when she got anywhere near the junior high part of her who was so overcome with pain and anguish, she did everything she could to stay away from the feelings. Sternly clamping down, the wounded part had no chance to tell her story and get better. However, now that the abused part is removed from evil, Trish can see a better ending for the abuse scene. "It is like I'm back. It's an entirely different movie."

Old movies can be deeply entrenched and hard to stop watching, but some are God-given, faith-producing movies. The husband of one person I'm helping, got to a "run down" place, and gave me a call. I asked him to come in so that I could see how he's doing. His world has been rocked by the pounding suffering that his wife has been going through, and there are times when he does not know how to help. Shortly after he arrived in my office that day, he told me that he believes things will turn out okay.

"Even if we lose our house God will help us into another one. Money is tight at this time, but there is some big money coming in soon, and I'm sure that we will make it."

"I really like the movie in your head," I said. "It has scenes that turn out right, even though they have uncertain spots in the middle. That is a movie on the Jesus channel. In those movies, God brings good out of everything. Please do not stop watching your movie. But you may have a problem if you try to convince your wife to watch your movie. Hers does not have very many scenes with good endings yet. Her movie is called, 'Growing Up in Hell.' Considering the serious abuse she suffered, there is no way that she is ready for a new movie, at least until her old movie gets some of the abuse scenes re-worked. All she can see right now are the horrid endings. Listen well to how she feels, but don't stop living the movie that God gives you. We need to keep working on her childhood scenes until they get some better endings. Her heart needs more healing before she will be ready to watch your movie."

I am hoping that some of the lessons I have learned will help her re-write her script.

7

Lessons about Healing Hearts

THERE IS A PROMINENT idea that is held onto very strongly in some Christian circles. Here is a characterization of that idea.

> When you come to Jesus, everything old is gone and life begins anew. Your past is past. Start over. You are a new person. You should be able to forget about any pain from the past. You only need to choose joy every day.

Have you heard that somewhere? I hope that you can you see the inherent flaw in that thinking. Here it is.

> Pain from the past is not truly *past* if you can still feel it. Only when it has been healed, is it *truly* past. However, if you cannot get over a lingering effect that interferes with your present, then it is *not* past. *It is present pain.* When a wound will not stop bringing you pain, you cannot simply ignore it. Either you will find healing, or it will make your day unmanageable. When you come to Jesus, He wants to help you put your present pain in the past by healing it.

An illustration will show how this works. A young man sought my help during the week after he had been taken captive in a car by some people wearing masks. He shortly escaped, and there was no physical harm, but some scenes from that evening would not stop replaying in his mind. Anxiety was making his life unmanageable. We went over everything that happened, moment by frightful moment, and for the first time he remembered all of the details. After we finished praying that God would heal everything that we uncovered, he said that he would be back for another visit with me, but he did not return. That was fine, because he got what he came for—the anxiety had received healing, and was now manageable. Getting the complete episode out on the table was needed so that it could be healed, and so that he could talk about it without being overwhelmed. He was able to go on with his life, unhindered.

God wants to provide healing for the wounds in your past that continue to bring you pain, so that you can allow him to guide you, *unhindered*, in your present. Feelings do not need to keep on interfering. When people come to Jesus, He wants to be with them right where they are, in the middle of their deepest struggle. That is what *The Beatitudes* are all about. "I will be with you when you need me." As you talk it all over with Him, He will help you get your life back on track.

But do not look for a "start over" button. There is none. You cannot unscramble eggs. People do not need a magician—they need a physician. *The Father wants to help all of us through our struggles, not just to simply make them go away.* Redemption is what God offers. It is a central idea in Christianity, and simply stated, it means that God brings good out of everything. Particularly when there is a large amount of pain, God wants to bring a lot of good out of it. Your story is not about pain. It is about how God works in the middle of your pain for your good. Scrambled eggs can be the start of a very fine omelet.

Healing is needed in order to be guided by the Father, or we will be guided by our wounds. When pain prevails[1] we are not free to be forgiving, genuine, peaceful, loving and sincere.[2] People seek my help because they are looking for freedom from the pain that blocks their life. Here is the essential ingredient for helping them with their pain—prayer for healing. We ask Him to help us open up the wound and then we ask Him to heal it. In order to seek His healing we need to know what to pray for. Identifying a wound is first. Then the whole story needs to be told—the wound is opened up in its painful reality. Prayer for healing follows, so that the pain can be drained. The wound will then no longer interfere, and the Father's guidance can again be followed, unhindered.

This chapter presents an overview of some lessons that I have been learning since I began to work with people at the heart level. The heart is where truth is either accepted or blocked, where God's guidance either

---

1. The first half of *The Sermon on the Mount* spells out how six areas of woundedness can misguide a person's life.

2. The second half of *The Sermon on the Mount* highlights that these traits flow from a transformed heart. They are evidence that a person bears the Father's family resemblance. That is what life is supposed to look like in the Kingdom of the Heavens.

flows into a life or it doesn't. It is where life finds its direction. The heart is where the "inside" is, when it comes to "living life from the inside out."

SPIRITUALLY BASED LESSONS

Restoring hearts so that they can receive God's direction is a central focus for Christian Counseling. I have been keeping that goal in mind for many years, and would like to contribute what I have been learning. A good place to begin is by reviewing the lessons that were mentioned in chapter 4, and explaining a little bit more about them.

1. *Wounds are psychological and they are spiritual.* People's suffering is incredibly deep, but they will open up about it if you give them a chance. They will get right into their most painful material, which will always have a spiritual side to it.

Sessions start in the right direction when they begin in prayer. We usually ask God for protection from the evil one, for guidance in everything that comes up, for help to not stick to our own plans, for filling by the Holy Spirit and for divine comfort. As He leads we may find that home issues come up, or there may be daunting internal pictures from the past or any number of unexpected stuck places. We will only know what we are going to work on after we turn the session over to the Father. We trust Him. He will bring good out of anything.

Wounds are deep, but they are always fairly close to the surface. People can identify them if given an opportunity. Many times the discovery process begins with finding the feeling that is interfering in the present, or one that has interfered recently. For example, if a person has become tearful on the way to see me, that is where we will begin to look. The tears are probably connected to a feeling that we will need to talk about, so that we can find the wound that needs prayer. The tears are coming from a physical or a psychological wound, and there also is some spiritual interference. Both need prayer. Wounds are real, and they really hurt. Satan's method is to isolate wounded people, and to bring intimidation and confusion into the picture, creating further damage for any wounds he can target.

Knowing that the mind is constantly working on feelings, and that they are close to the surface, gives me an accurate starting place for every session. We do not have to go through a family history and place our guesses about what is going on. Instead, we talk about the most recent time when a feeling interfered, and "climb back into that moment," to allow the feeling to emerge more fully. The brain is always working on feelings, and when the intrusive feelings emerge it is necessary to remember that the reason the feelings are coming up is because they want to get better! Many, many people believe that feelings are the problem, and they need to be stuffed away, but that is not the case. Actually, if people keep stuffing feelings, they will not get better and the feelings will become even more of a problem. When we climb back into the moment to get in touch with the painful feeling, we are doing what we can to get the feeling expressed, so that we will know what to pray for. When a wound has received healing, Satan loses a target to inflict further damage. That is crucial in finding resolution.

2. *Spiritual attacks are to be expected whenever pain is exposed.* The enemy's lies are about never getting better, not being good enough or being fatally flawed, or there may be some other spiritual stronghold that needs a prayerful time of "working through," in order to break the lies.

Many times the spiritual interference is a "stronghold"—a lie that will not let go. The lie can be planted during a trauma, and sometimes there is a vow or a curse in the trauma that drives the lie deeper. The resulting stronghold plays out, scene after scene, in the person's inner movie. There may be a demonic attachment, which means there are spiritual issues involved that make the wound even more entrenched. But even without demons, strongholds tell people how to live in ways that pull them away from God's guidance. "You are cruel, just like your father," is a lie that could use some prayer.

> The weapons we fight with have divine power to break strongholds. We take every thought captive and make it obedient to Christ.[3] You are not like your earthly father. That lie is busted. God's truth can guide you from now on, and here is the truth: You are created in His image and He designed you to do good works, which He will help you accomplish.[4]

Whenever a lie is exerting too much influence, it usually means that the lie is the aftereffect of a trauma. For example, one person told me that marriage is like being a sex slave. My response was that it makes sense, based on the movie in her head, to believe that. Her first husband was dominating and abusive, so what else would her movie script show

3. This is taken from 2 Corinthians chapter 10.

4. This comes from Ephesians 2:10.

her? After revisiting the kind of episode where that man abused her, and praying for healing, we also asked God to help her rewrite her script. She immediately knew that this is the way to go. Her inner movie is based on a lie. God intended marriage to be a source of strength and joy, and she will need to keep on reworking scenes that perpetuate the lie, as she moves ahead in her life.

3. *Beware of quick fixes.* Deep suffering opens up over a long period of time, and we need God's patience while attending to it, until it is properly relieved. Too often, the immediate relief of some pain feels so wonderfully "blessed by God," that a person will hope everything is suddenly okay. "I'm done. God is done, and I'm doing great!" It makes more sense to persist in seeking His guidance for as long as healing of particular wounds is still underway.

Certain feelings are completely intolerable. Anxiety and rage are most offensive, and a person cannot stay in those for very long. Something has to be done immediately to make them go away. Very offensive feelings can come up when a person is working on a wound from the past, particularly a wound that contains hopelessness, contempt or lust. It is impossible for a person to endure the feelings that come from those wounds for even a few minutes. These questions are often heard. "When will I be done with this? How long until I'm back to normal? Do I really have to deal with this pain?"

It takes determination and faith to work through some wounds, and it takes people who are encouraging. Hearts can easily be turned aside from the healing pathway. The gate is narrow. Managing feelings can seem good enough when pain is intense. That gate is much wider. The Father's guidance will lead to the right gate.

4. *Spiritual attacks should be expected.* Counselors' every fear, weakness, conflict and character flaw will be targeted by Satan. He does not want this work to succeed. Those on the front lines will take personal hits, and so will their families. This is not intended for beginners, nor for the faint of heart. A strong faith, along with a year or two of steady training and prayer support is a minimum. As Paul put it, we are afflicted in every way but not crushed, perplexed but not driven to despair, persecuted but not forsaken, struck down but not destroyed (2 Corinthians 4:8–9). Those who persist will depend on the Father's companionship while the battle is

being fought. As each battle comes to an end, we find that God has been steadily at work bringing good out of it.

Satan is very threatened by people who thwart his work. He promotes isolation, confusion, chaos and death. The weak and the wounded are his targets, and people who protect his targets are his enemy. Expect interference in the areas where you are weak. You will find it necessary to stay strong in the Lord and to keep seeking His help for your weaknesses, or you will find yourself turning away in despair.

People need to be spiritual warriors for the right reasons. If it is mostly an ego trip, destruction will result sooner or later. There is no hall of fame for people who have taken satanic hits. We have all had our share. The key in overcoming those hits is to recognize them. Recognizing and praying about them are best accomplished in small groups or in mentoring relationships. In the scripture mentioned above we are assured that God will be faithful when we take a hit. Faith grows, and so does a person's confidence, as God brings good out of these painful, spiritual encounters.

5. *Ask God to help you to grow in the area of discernment.* We each need to learn to recognize Satan's interference as it comes against us, and to rely on the power of God. Remember that when Jesus sent out his disciples He mentioned that they would face demons, so we should not be surprised to find ourselves in spiritual battles. There is no splendor, nor anything to brag about when it comes to winning spiritual battles. It is ugly and the only good part is when the present battle is over. A seasoned warrior waits for orders, knows where the power comes from and uses it wisely. The battle is the Lord's.

Someone in my Bible study group recently asked how to pray for me. "Please pray that I will be incompetent, more effectively," was my immediate answer. That pretty well sums it up. My ideas and my power are not where the help comes from. It had better not be me against Satan. It is the power of God that brings people out of the pit and plants their feet on the rock. If there is victory, He gets the praise and we are blessed to watch Him work. People who volunteer for training in spiritual warfare should be those who need help with the battles that they are already in, not those who are interested in seeing the Devil defeated. It is better to fight the battles that come to us rather than to seek battles, or to observe other people's battles. We need to wait for His orders.

6. *Learn to trust God's faithfulness.* When two or more are gathered for prayer, God is in their midst. He will not only show up, but He will deliver from evil and will often provide an inspiring sense of joy as the session closes.

During my two years of training in spiritual warfare I was forced to learn the same dramatic lesson many times, namely, that hopelessness is Satan's trademark. When I am certain in my gut that we have opened up an unfixable wound, that means Satan is bearing down. Hopelessness is trying to take over. When the battle revolves around hopelessness and my feelings lose their way, that suggests there is a spiritual battle afoot. Sensing the hopelessness helps me to pray more effectively. As we continue to follow His leading, He answers, and we join with Him in celebration. He is faithful. Joy is His trademark.

7. *Spiritual lessons apply everywhere.* God wants to pour out His blessing at times other than scheduled prayer sessions. His intention is to do this kind of work during every hour of the day, in and out of the office.

My father, a retired pastor, used to teach about the church gathered, and the church scattered. I found that approach to life helped me a lot. We are God's people, twenty-four, seven. He creates a certain kind of experience for us while we are gathered in His name, imparts to us His strength while we are there, and He accompanies us back into the world until we meet again. We can expect His power to be present in every area of our life, as opposed to thinking about His power dwelling in church, or in a place of prayer. Of course, it is wonderful to be the church gathered. Crucial moments happen there, and it truly strengthens us. As we gather it helps us to be the church more effectively when we scatter, to do His work. We are reminded of who we are when we are gathered, and the worship and teaching promote His work in our lives as we go our separate ways.

That is the kind of thinking that I try to promote in my office. People work through the carried-over feelings from painful events, they change in some very real spiritual and psychological ways, and they bring the changes along with them as they move into the rest of their life. It goes the other way too—changes that God brings into their lives while they are away from my office can be brought back to share with me. His work is certainly not limited to a few hours in my office each week or to a few hours in church each Sunday. God wants to be involved all of the time. I consider my work to be a boost for those who pray with me, and I consider their church involvement to be a boost, but God wants to join people in every arena of their life.

Usually people have about three arenas in which they live their lives. There is home, church and there is usually one other arena, like their career or the gym or a restaurant, like a sports team, a weight loss program, a computer-based reality or a home Bible study group. God wants to be involved wherever you go, not only in the church arena. His companionship will help in every arena of your life, if you invite Him to stay with you in your living space.

A FEW OTHER LESSONS

8. *There are two kinds of pain that show up in traumatic memories—abuse and neglect.* Prayer for healing episodes of abuse, which includes violence of every sort, is most often a case where praying for healing involves a single event. Neglect is what happens when a whole chapter of life is full of "needs not being met." But neglect can also happen when a whole chapter of life is full of repeated abuse, and that may be in addition to "needs not being met." As a result, this means that prayer for the healing of neglect wounds is usually different than prayer for healing abuse wounds.

Prayer for neglect responds more gradually than prayer for abuse, since there is so much more painful time involved, and there are often more episodes of violence that were inflicted during the periods of neglect. Steady prayer and support are needed to keep progress going. The only way to know whether you are praying for healing of abuse or neglect is to start praying. It will only become evident just how much damage was done as you get into the prayer process. It may be that a single abuse episode is all that will come up during a person's story, but some people's stories will be surprisingly full of painful episodes. That is where the Father's guidance is essential.

Let your prayers and the telling of the painful stories be guided by the Father who is right beside you. You will not have to figure out in advance what to pray for. The pain that you find close to the surface is what you will pray for. That particular pain, whether it is abuse-based or neglect-based, is coming up because it wants to get healed. Tell the story and pray for healing.

Most cases of heart hurt come from neglect. Hopelessness is certainly neglect-based. The memories that lead to hopelessness are usually repeated abusive episodes. A sizable chapter of life will have that kind of pain in it, and the conclusion reached there, that things will always be bad, is a lie that is not easily broken until the pain is resolved. That is what makes hopelessness so hard to beat. Prayer for healing one episode of abuse may make a difference in hopelessness, but if the hopelessness is also connected to other abuse episodes, they will also need some prayer before the hopelessness can be fully healed.

It is particularly important to understand the difference between prayer for abuse and prayer for neglect, when people come for prayer following a church service. People with abuse wounds may feel joyful right away after prayer, since that can happen at times when only a single event needs healing. But when neglect is the problem, people can not only become discouraged at the lack of immediate joy, but they can falsely conclude that there is something terribly wrong with them because they do not feel much better soon after prayer. That is when it is good to encourage them to think about it like this: Healing has really happened, but there may be other wounds that are not yet healed. It is also good to encourage them to seek support from family and friends, as their healing continues.

9. *Support is essential.* Talk about your story and about your healing with friends and family. It may take quite a while to heal your heart, so seek a lot of support.

Perhaps we can look at lust as an example. Recently, there has been increasing attention to helping people overcome lust, along with associated pornography addiction problems. It is becoming clear that it works pretty well to treat lust like an addiction, and to treat it in a group setting. The "12 Step" approach seems to fit pretty well. Those meetings begin with the declaration that we will need God's help if we are going to win the lust battle, and it includes that we will need to tell our story in a supportive environment. Support is essential, or the person will certainly return to the addiction.

Hopelessness, contempt and the other heart areas mentioned in *The Sermon on the Mount* also progress better when there is a chance to receive support from those who know how hard the battle is, and when their support remains in place for a long time. As was the case with lust, prayer for the healing of any memories that result in heart woundedness will be beneficial.[5] Individual counseling or family-related counseling or a Christian-based 12 step program may be very helpful in cleansing your heart so that you can live from it. Sharing your story so that you can receive healing prayer is essential. God helps you and He helps those who pray for you as well.

Here is one more reason why we need to be supportive. Family and friends are as essential for life as oxygen. As is discussed more fully in *The Life Model*, we need each other in order to make progress in maturity, throughout our life. Common, serious blockages in life result from neglect in childhood, but these can be overcome in adulthood. The deficiencies that came from childhood neglect can be filled in with the help of the family of God. When the family of God is working as it should, brothers and sisters, fathers and mothers and extended family members boost each other along to make up for the good that we did not receive in childhood. The fundamental need being met is belonging. When we belong to a family that boosts our maturity, we will be more successful in following His guidance.[6]

10. *Safety and protection are essential.* In order for healing to progress, the person's living environment needs to be supportive. People at home need to be in alignment with, and attuned to, the healing process. That means providing nurture and recovery time whenever needed, and it means asking how to become involved as well as when to back off.

Family and friends should take a non-confrontive approach, and seek to learn about their role in promoting recovery. A huge complication often comes up when the victim's parents have been the abusers. Even while living away from offending parents, there is too often a hope for reconciliation that exceeds realistic thinking. Many abusers would go to jail, or at least would have their world seriously rocked if evidence about their abuse were disclosed. Of children who have been abused, it has been estimated that 90% of them have been threatened or coerced in some way, to maintain their silence. Abusive people will go to any length to hide

---

5. Six areas are mentioned in the first half of *The Sermon on the Mount.* chapter 2 in this book contains details.

6. *II Peter*, chapter 1 uses phrases like "ineffective and unproductive" and "nearsighted and blind" for people who do not possess certain qualities that involve seeking maturity "in increasing measure." Peter's idea is that it is up to us to work on goodness, knowledge, self-control, perseverance, godliness, brotherly kindness and love. God cannot simply hand those to us.

their guilt, and that includes continuing intimidation, manipulation and abuse well into adulthood. It is always a struggle to know when to give up on the hope that an offending parent will repent. The Father's guidance is really a key in all of this, but most likely, abusive parents will not repent, and will continue to be defensive or offensive. That works against safety and protection, particularly if regular contact is expected. The resulting confrontations, legal battles and family uproar do not help at all in recovery. People can usually learn how to maintain safe boundaries with offensive parents, and they pray that God will bless the offending parents, but they also learn to protectively keep away from dangerous people, even parents.

Here is the guideline that I try to keep in mind, since it makes such a monumental difference in recovery: The person's living environment needs to support the healing work, or it will not progress. In cases where this guideline is not followed, people often feel better after a session but they are thrown back into their pain when they return home, and the progress disappears. This is why I try to set aside some time during each session to talk about keeping family life in alignment with the recovery process.

11. *It's all about parts and wounds.* Even though this sounds overly simplified, it turns out that for practically all those who seek my help, this is exactly what we end up working on, no matter where we begin. Whether the person's concern is about anxiety, marriage problems, depression or addictions, I end up hearing, "Sometimes I feel this way and sometimes I don't. Part of me wants to stay and part of me is outta' here." People need to get God into every area of their life, particularly to help heal any wounds (see the first half of *The Sermon on the Mount*) that interfere with living from a transformed heart (see the second half). It makes sense that Jesus' brother, James, began his biblical letter with a plea for people to get real about their dividedness.[7]

Examples abound. Without warning, a person may completely break down in tears, fly off in a brutal rage, "start drinking again," flirt with infidelity or may suddenly act in ways which do not seem anything like the person they really are. It's all about parts and wounds. When a person lives from their hurt, which is where the unexpected, interrupting behaviors come from, they cannot live from a heart that is attuned to God. Wounds need to be healed and parts need to be unified in order to overcome the interruptions.

---

7. See the first 8 verses in James.

For people whose abuse began during their preschool years, the dividedness may take the form of dissociation. I have learned much about this condition through providing therapy for more than 100 such people.[8] Typically they have been misdiagnosed and blamed, because they have not received proper assistance to understand and overcome the effects of the early abuse. One serious problem often arises because counselors and friends falsely believe that the person who dissociates can stop the switching if they *try* harder. But here is the stark truth: Dissociation is involuntary—it kicks in before the "switch in personalities" can be stopped. Stated another way, the change from one personality part to another happens before the person can choose to stop it. When therapy begins, trying to stop going back-and-forth between personality parts is much like trying to prevent a knee-jerk reaction. However, with healing and unification, the effects are overcome. For their whole life, people who dissociate have endured unnecessary blame for not "choosing" to do better. Since dissociation is involuntary—automatic—the blame is not only undeserved, but the blame blocks healing by keeping the story hidden. Understanding and receiving the appropriate help are essential to overcome the wounds that led to dissociation in the first place. As is the case for others in recovery, dissociative people are splendid folks who carry around a burden. When wounds are healed and parts are unified, the burden can be dropped and they are free to live from a transformed heart.

12. *A split heart makes life unlivable.* Unfinished abuse and neglect can lead people to live with their intentions, their passions and their deepest motivations going in two contradictory directions. When the heart splits right down the middle, depression sets in, the support of friends dwindles, and there is a stronger sense than ever that life is an unending ride on a vicious merry-go-round. Feelings that got their start because of abuse and neglect can be managed, just barely, for a short period of time, and then the unhealed feelings take over again. Back-and-forth, neither direction in life seems to fit. Perhaps a "split heart" is easy to recognize when relationships separate, time and again, yet re-unite each time. Here is what a woman told me.

---

8. My goal has been to educate counselors, people who dissociate, and friends of those who dissociate by writing two books, *Uncovering the Mystery of MPD* and *More than Survivors: Conversations with Multiple Personality Clients*, and in presenting more than 100 seminars.

"The Bible says that God hates divorce, and I am trusting that God will bring my husband back. I believe that He can do anything. My friends tell me about miracles where God completely changes a man even when he has been away from God for years. My husband has been having an affair and has left me, yet I believe that if I keep committing to prayer and to the marriage, God can still work things out. But I cry myself to sleep every night, I'm taking antidepressants again and I can hardly handle my job. I am dead if I lose my job. My friends say that I've got to have more faith. I've got to keep going but I keep falling apart."

That is a common tale, but true, to use an old *cliché*. Support groups exist for people whose hearts are split in exactly that way. Some of the people can manage their feelings pretty well because they receive the proper support from their group, while other people completely fall apart. It seems that those whose hearts are split most deeply have abuse and neglect spoiling their childhoods, and the movie in their head is playing the same hopeless scenes over and over again. For split hearts that will not stop hurting, there needs to be healing for past and present wounds, and there needs to be a way to avoid the torture of being constantly reminded that "my husband is still having an affair."

Here is what makes sense to me: First, this woman needs to settle the question about whether her husband is coming back. Remember, God wants him to do the right thing, but cannot direct his heart. It is, sadly, out of God's hands. The woman mentioned above is saying that she is trusting God to bring her husband back, but she is actually trusting that her husband can return to her and can change into an honest person, even though he is living a lie. As long as she goes back-and-forth between hope and hurt, she will keep falling apart pretty often. If it can be settled that he is not coming back, then her living environment can attain enough safety to seek some healing, without having her wounds repeatedly torn open. Only then can the wounds from past and present can get properly attended to. God hates divorce, but when it happens, He loves to see His children healed and living from a unified heart. He must have something better for them.

As was suggested in the "It's all about parts and wounds" lesson, "split heart" is a widespread condition. A heart tells you how to live—it directs your life. For people whose lives are sometimes directed by addictions, by unhealthy relationships, by sexual urges or for people who go back-and-forth about their faith in God, it makes sense to me that they will not rise above their *problem* while their heart remains split.

13. *Joy is stronger than fear.* You surely have seen toddlers scampering across the room with arms wide open, soon to be scooped up by the one they love. Their faces are aglow. And you may have seen people singing praises to God with all of their might, with arms lifted up, enjoying the one they love with all of their heart. Those are scenes in which joy is displayed in its full power. Joy comes from expecting to be with your beloved, and it reaches its peak while you are with your beloved. Love leads to joy, and joy comes from love. That is so sweet an experience, that every ounce of a person's resources can be organized around being with the beloved. Being caught up in joy is a very strong pull.

But fear can be pretty strong too. Especially for people who have been seeking healing for wound after wound, fear can seem as though it will prevail. It may even seem that life is an endless line of painful days waiting to be endured. Despair, meaninglessness, emptiness and hopelessness come from too great an exposure to pain. Fear says that there will be no relief.

But that is not what scientists say, and that is not what the Lord says. Scientists say that when pain blockages are sorted out, the mind will automatically return to joy. Joy is the natural state of affairs. The mind knows that, and that is why all of a person's resources are devoted to joy. "The joy of the Lord is my strength," is a resounding line in a song from King David. Everything within us counts on joy. When pain blockages have been worked through, when Satan's lies have been eliminated, and when the family of God supports those who suffer, joy will prevail. We are created in the image of God, which means that our deepest desire is to be in love, and to be directed by joy. If given any chance at all, even the most deeply wounded people will find that joy can direct them. It is as though each of us has been born with an inner compass that will always point to joy. Keep on believing that as you stick to the basics—finding healing, breaking lies and providing family-of-God support—joy will prove to be stronger than fear.

14. *Learning about healing is a life-long adventure.* The world over, there are advances being discovered regularly about healing, and about how to overcome wounds, from the everyday varieties to the extreme. There will always be room to develop more advanced clinical skills by

those who are serious about helping others. There will always be new, exciting material in science and in brain research. There will never be a "perfect" level of spiritual maturity that you or I will reach. Each one of us has a long way to go in all three areas. The longer we remain committed to the adventure, the better we will become in helping others. There are many lessons ahead, so please keep on encouraging and challenging each other. The Father will guide us, and that means we can expect to do better.

STAYING ON THE NARROW PATHWAY

Now that you and I are approaching the conclusion of our conversation, please do not let me suggest that there will only be joyful days ahead for you if you do this or that, nor that your story will be effortless from now on if you are a nice person. Life will always be difficult, and each day will bring you new challenges. But more to the point, here is a truth that you will not be able to avoid: Pain and suffering are closely linked with life. If you seek a life that rises above pain and suffering, you will surely need the Father working closely with you in your living space, when times get desperate.

Times will get desperate. It has been about seventeen years now, since my first book was released. I was due for quite a surprise the moment it was published. People began to call me on the phone or to write to me about their problems, as though I would know something suitable for their predicament. Counselors would call and tell me about the person they are trying to help, for whom nothing works. Of course, I have tried to help when that is possible, but through it all I have found that there are many people with huge problems and few resources out there. So many folks are without hope. Terror, nightmares, anxiety that will not stop, recurring illnesses which have no cause, spiritual vows and curses that keep coming back, counselors who make big mistakes and only seek help after the damage has been done—the list is endless. People all over the world face brutal issues and unworkable living conditions. Many suffering people have completely given up, but others are still seeking answers. Pastors are left without guidelines, and counselors are clueless to find ideas that provide some hope when there are no answers, no matter how thoroughly they have been trained.

This chapter presents some lessons that can help you to find the right path. But even then, there are people whose lives seem to be running along a different path. When people get stuck, it seems as though many pastors and counselors get too complicated with their interventions, or they try to come up with something new if nothing works. I have found that it's always back to the basics. Please do not look for a new guru, nor seek some obscure Bible verse, nor hope for a miracle solution. I believe that when people get off the main path, they need to get back on it. Following are four basic ideas that point in the right direction. But first, here is another truth that you will not be able to avoid: Talk everything over with the Father, especially when you are stuck. It will require His helping hand to stay on the right pathway. It will take His guidance to make these ideas suit your predicament, when times are desperate.

1. *Live safely.* In order for counseling to progress as it should, family life needs to support the on-going emotional work. Recovery sometimes requires climbing a steep mountain of pain, and planting God's flag on the peak before skiing down the other side. Climbing is best done when team members are always available to provide extra attention to serious wounds. In cases where extended family members or other "friends" work against the team, they need to be excluded. The unfriendly clatter can become a little too loud, blocking the Father's voice.

Living safely can be hard to accomplish, especially when people do not know how to get off of the merry-go-round where they have been wounded so many times. There is no precise formula. It is important to keep all fourteen lessons in mind, and to seek God's healing for the wounds that keep people stuck. Even then, people can believe that they will never be able to move ahead. That is exactly where Jesus began His sermon. Here is what we heard Jesus saying in *The Beatitudes*.

> I can tell how hard life is for you. You may believe that God will never pour out His goodness onto you in any meaningful way. Trust me. You can live a far better life if you open up to His presence. He is always available to help you, especially during hard times. When you are spiritually broken, overcome with sadness, treated unfairly, trying to live a better life, seriously drained, deeply longing, overwhelmed and persecuted, be encouraged—God is at work all around you. Your heart does not need to stay troubled. Let yourself enjoy His presence. It is wonderful to be with the Father. By welcoming Him into your living space, you will enter into the Kingdom of the Heavens.

He will help you to safely make it through the day. As Jesus added in the "Peacefulness and Your Heart" section, you can drop your worries.

It all comes down to believing that the Father will take care of you. Do not worry at all about tomorrow, even though you could find enough evil to worry about in every "tomorrow" if you tried. Drop your worries. You can count on Him to take care of you. (Matthew 6:34)

2. *Develop a routine that meets all of your needs.* For people who are depressed, desperate or simply worn out, attention should be paid to this guideline. Daily strength and coping power depend on this. Eating properly, at the same time each day, not only gives the body its required nutrients, but it plays a big role in letting the body know when it should be sleepy. If your eating schedule is steady, that will help with your sleeping schedule, and that will help with your depression. Similarly, if spiritual strength is sought only once each week or less than that, God's power will seem completely absent. Folks who are struggling can benefit from a steady diet of physical and spiritual nourishment in their daily routines.

It is clear that if God is to be active in your living space, He needs to be included as a customary part of your routine. Talk to Him as the day begins, whenever you move between the arenas of your life, whenever you prepare to speak with someone and whenever there are *surprises* in your day. The *surprise* may at first appear to be an interruption but may actually be a blessing, so be patient with your day and find out what unexpected goodness He has for you. There should be a balance among the arenas of your life. Too much church, work, play or too much staying at home each has its downside. Isolation is a problem, but so is over-involvement in any arena of life. It sometimes helps people to schedule their day, hour by hour, in order to keep paying the right kind of attention to each need. When the routine fails, there is often too much commotion, and the Father's voice is hard to recognize.

How the day begins can make a huge difference in each day's success or failure. I often inquire about how people start their day. Pattie told me that she never had been asked about that before, but she has found a great way to begin her day. She told me that on days where she remembers to do this, which is about half of the time, she sings some praise music and then pictures herself on a kind of platform. On one side is God the Father and Jesus is on the other side. She bows to each and asks them to be with her. Then she's "good to go." The singing and the visual are vital for this woman. Other people read scripture or find particular ways to spend their quiet time with God. Getting Him into the beginning of the day helps a lot. Here is a particularly popular approach. Getting alone is essential, while thinking about each of the day's activities. Then asking God for guidance in each activity makes sense, and only then can the day get a successful start.

Again we see that there is no formula. Here is what we hear Jesus saying in *The Lord's Prayer*: The key to making it all work is talking about every part of your day with the Father. You will either talk about these areas with the Father as they come up in your daily life, or you will fail to put Jesus' teaching into practice. Your heart will need some gentle assistance as each day unfolds, so you will find that His companionship is essential.

3. *In with the good and out with the bad.* It helps to keep progressing in both areas—filling up with the good and forcing out the bad. Try to steer clear of people and movements that emphasize only the good or the bad. On the filling side of the equation, setting aside times for worship, prayer, study of the Bible, solitude and corporate praise are all wonderful disciplines that can keep a life properly filled.[9] However, all of the "filling up with good" that you can handle will not push out the evil. It sneaks into your life, so you could use some help identifying it and keeping it out. Not only is it good to stay away from addictive activities and avoid using chemicals that send you out-of-control, but there may be times when you should expel demonic interference, and stay away from "bad" people. Remember that unhealed wounds can get nastily stirred up by demonic activity, so the healing of wounds and expelling of demons often go hand in hand.[10] Spiritual warfare should be available to properly push out the bad whenever it appears.

When I asked Wally how he begins his day, he said that he gets up fairly early so that he has enough time for devotions. He said he reads a passage from the Old Testament, then a Psalm, a bit from the Gospels and something from the Epistles. Then he says *the Lord's Prayer* and adds a spontaneous prayer, to cover everything in his life, and he reads a daily devotional which wraps it up. As Wally was telling me about all of this it seemed that his devotions are about as thorough as I could imagine. The

---

9. *Disciplines of the Holy Spirit*, by Siang-Yang Tan and Douglas Gregg, and *The Spirit of the Disciplines*, by Dallas Willard are good resources.

10. *Uncovering the Mystery of MPD* provides a section which includes spiritual warfare and how to tell the difference between evil spirits and wounded personality states. *Christianity with Power*, by Charles H. Kraft, is another good resource for finding healing in the spiritual warfare arena.

next question seemed obvious to me, but caught him quite by surprise. I asked whether he prays at other times during the day. No. Without being consciously aware of it, he had kind of learned to fill up on God at the start of the day, and had come to expect that will take care of everything.

My next thought was to find out about the rest of his day. He is a teacher, so we found that in addition to the "spiritual part" of him, there is a "teacher part," a "home improvement" part, a "father part" and a "husband part." After he drives to work and gets out of his car, he readies his classroom and does not think about God. When he stops by the lumber yard on his way home, he does not think about God. The same is true when he is with his kids, when he is with his wife, and it is particularly true when he gets near the sexual area of life. Thinking it all through with me, Wally got the picture: It is great to begin the day all filled up with God, but it also makes sense to keep talking with God throughout the day, as he sets up his classroom, and as he moves into each of the other arenas of his life. Within three weeks he had realized that there was something in his sexual life that was not responding properly to the prayer, but everything else was going better, now that God was being invited into each part of the day. We found some hidden memories of sexual abuse at a boarding school during his Junior High years, and prayer for healing that wound was needed. We also decided to cast out the spirit that was interfering with his sexual life. I am not certain whether our work created the kind of progress that Wally and his wife were looking for, but the work we did together seemed about right. It was mostly about getting God into every part of his life, and getting the evil out as well. There seemed to be attention paid to both letting the good in and to getting the bad out. I believe that he was ready to live from a transformed heart.

4. *Live from your heart, and not from your hurt.* This may not be as simple as it sounds. I know of a person who was constantly criticized where she lived. Much of the time she found herself being either defensive or she was in tears. Her living environment practically required her to live from her hurt while at home. No wonder she had a hard time feeling like herself. Her heart was being pushed out of the picture, from her first waking moments each morning. She needed to start her recovery by talking things over with the Father. That is always appropriate in sorting out problems, and it gives people strength to climb their mountain. He led her to move away from her friends, into a safer setting. Getting off to a safe

start each day was essential for her, in order to stay away from the hurt that so easily can direct her life. When people begin the day in their heart, the Father's voice is much clearer.

Another person went in and out of a hurt place quite often, without realizing that she was living from her hurt. One time when we began to talk she could not get away from saying, "I'm ugly." Her husband was with us during every session, and he and I could not convince her that she certainly was not ugly. Our logic completely failed to convince her. Nothing worked. We went in the right direction when we began to trace just where that comment was coming from. A very young part of her had been frozen in time because of extreme abuse, and that part of her had been ridiculed for being ugly, during the abuse. Of course, the frozen, young part believed it was true, even though as an adult she looked quite the opposite. Prayer for healing and deliverance were both helpful, and thereafter she did not need to feel ugly. The wound had been healed, and she was able to live from the inside out, from her heart. That is a much better movie.

Particularly when people are anxious, they can say things and do things that are out of character. Later they will become aware that they were living in their hurt. But anxiety is not the only problem area. Defensiveness, anger, making hasty decisions and acting impetuously are some other ways that people get stuck living in their hurt. Another example is "getting triggered." A former soldier may duck and cover whenever a loud noise is heard, or a woman may go numb whenever touched by a man. Triggers leap up and take control. That is another way that people can get stuck living in their hurt. Triggers can instantly produce hopelessness, contempt, lust, dishonesty, retaliation or false righteousness. Jesus' sermon was about all of these. Here is the most helpful perspective: Whenever a trigger comes up it is a chance to seek healing for a troublesome wound. View it as an opportunity to make progress, and not just as another reminder that you are on a merry-go-round. After the hurt has been healed, you will be able to jump off and return to a life that is lived from your heart.

Living from a transformed heart happens when your wounds have been healed, and the Father is invited to direct your daily life. A new person begins to emerge, one who bears the Father's likeness. He is at hand, ready to pour out a blessing, and to help you climb your mountain. Forgiveness, genuineness, peacefulness and sincerity become more prominent, and relationships naturally take on the qualities of love. The urge within your soul to live a far better life is being steadily satisfied. Keep talking with the Father about staying on the pathway that He has for you. You are ready to participate in the Kingdom of the Heavens.

A Postlude

WALKING IN A REDWOOD grove reveals a world that exists in a different light. It takes a few minutes for a person's eyes to fully adjust. There is a ceiling effect that is created by a canopy of the upper redwood branches, high overhead, which blocks out most of the direct sunlight. The absence of the sun's rays makes life impossible for smaller trees, and for many of the flowering plants and bushes that need photosynthesis. As a result, the ground-hugging forms of life are missing, and the trails do not get crowded out by competing vegetation. Velvet-like columns silently support the ceiling, and the floor remains mostly clear, except for a few gigantic fallen branches. Clutter is practically gone. Soft light prevails, so in this world there are no hidden corners and there is nothing demanding a spotlight. The living environment has its own way of spreading illumination, and pointing out what to look at.

Life in the Kingdom of the Heavens is a lot like that. The Father's companionship allows you to take an uncluttered look at your life. Nothing needs to remain hidden. He has a way of telling you what to look at. Chill. Take it all in. Talk everything over with Him.

Jesus' teaching is simple but following it requires clear-headed determination. In case you are serious about turning every area of your life over to Him, that means you are willing to look at whatever He shows you. It may be that on church days you believe that you have turned everything over to Him, but what about the other days, and what about the wounded feelings that spill out at times? Is it a breeze to give Him your hopelessness, contempt, lust, dishonesty, retaliation and false righteousness? It may be tough. His companionship will be needed to find all of your wounds and to face them. There are no hidden corners. But do not give up. Turning every area of your life over to Him is what happens in the Kingdom of the Heavens. Be ready to give it some time and effort. Forgiveness, genuineness, peacefulness, sincerity and loving relationships are worth it. The first chapter of *James* says that a lack of faith keeps people divided—tossed to and fro like a wave in the wind. Getting faith into every area of your life makes all the difference in the world. You will need to talk about your heart's desires with Him throughout each day, especially when wounded feelings are around, and be willing to look at whatever He shows you. That is how to get His help into the areas of your life that could use some healing, into the areas darkened by lies, and into the areas that have not yet taken the first step—inviting Him to be with you in life's most difficult moments.

Trust that He will help you to stay on the pathway. Your heart does not need to remain troubled. Ask Him to heal your wounds. He wants to be very active in your living space, providing guidance so that you can live from a transformed heart.

References

Anderson, Neil T. *The Bondage Breaker.* Harvest House. Eugene, Oregon, 1990.

Bailey, Kenneth Ewing. *Poet and Peasant: A literary–Cultural Approach to the Parables in Luke.* Eerdmans Publishing. Grand Rapids, Michigan, 1976.

Bennett, Rita. *You Can Be Emotionally Free.* Bridge-Logos Publishers. Alachua, Florida, 1982.

Bruce, F. F. *The Hard Sayings of Jesus.* InterVarsity Press. Downers Grove, Illinois, 1983.

Flynn, Kathryn A. *The Sexual Abuse of Women by Members of the Clergy.* McFarland Publishers. Jefferson, North Carolina, 2003.

Fortune, Marie M. *Is Nothing Sacred?* United Church Press. Cleveland, Ohio, 1989.

Friesen, James G. *Uncovering the Mystery of MPD.* Wipf & Stock Publishers. Eugene, Oregon, 1991.

———. *More Than Survivors: Conversations With Multiple-Personality Clients.* Wipf & Stock Publishers, 1992.

———. Wilder, E. James; Bierling, Anne M.; Koepcke, Rick & Poole, Maribeth. *The Life Model: Living from the Heart Jesus Gave You.* Shepherd's House, Inc. Pasadena, California, 2000.

Johnson, Hank. *They Felled the Redwoods.* Stauffer Publishing. Fish Camp, California, 1996.

Kraft, Charles H. *Christianity with Power.* Servant Publications. Ann Arbor, Michigan, 1989.

Los Angeles County Commission for Women, Ritual Abuse Task Force. *Ritual Abuse: Definitions, Glossary, The Use of Mind Control.* Los Angeles, California, 1994.

Malony, H. Newton and Augsburger, David S. *Christian Counseling: An Introduction.* Abingdon Press. Nashville, 2007.

Miller, Dee Ann. *How Little We Knew: Collusion and Confession with Sexual Misconduct.* Prescott Press. Lafayette, Louisiana, 1993.

Payne, Leanne. *The Healing Presence.* Crossway Books. Wheaton, Illinois, 1989.

Perez, Pamela. *Just Before Dawn.* Author House. Bloomingdale, Indiana, 2003.

San Diego County Commission on Children & Youth, Ritual Abuse Task Force. *Ritual Abuse: Treatment, Intervention and Safety Guidelines.* San Diego, California, 1991.

Schore, Allan N. *The Science of the Art of Psychotherapy.* UCLA David Geffen School of Medicine, February 2–3, 2007.

Tan, Siang-Yang and Gregg, Douglas H. *Disciplines of the Holy Spirit.* Zondervan, Grand Rapids, Michigan, 1997.

U.S. Department of Health and Human Services Administration for Children and Families. *A Nation's Shame: Fatal Child Abuse and Neglect in the United States. A Report of the U.S. Advisory Board on Child Abuse and Neglect.* Fifth Report, April, 1995.

Willard, Dallas. *The Divine Conspiracy: Rediscovering Our Hidden Life in God.* HarperCollins Publishers. New York, New York, 1998.

———. *Hearing God: Developing a Conversational Relationship with God.* Intervarsity Press. Downers Grove, Illinois, 1999.

———. *The Spirit of the Disciplines: Understanding How God Changes Lives.* HarperCollins, New York, 1988.